Forever Free

THE STORY OF THE
EMANCIPATION PROCLAMATION

Other books by Dorothy Sterling

BROWNIE SCOUT MYSTERY

CAPTAIN OF THE PLANTER
The Story of Robert Smalls

CATERPILLARS

CREATURES OF THE NIGHT

THE CUB SCOUT MYSTERY

FREEDOM TRAIN
The Story of Harriet Tubman

INSECTS AND THE HOMES THEY BUILD

MARY JANE

SECRET OF THE OLD POST-BOX

UNITED NATIONS, N.Y.

THE SILVER SPOON MYSTERY

THE STORY OF CAVES

THE STORY OF MOSSES, FERNS, AND MUSHROOMS

TREES AND THEIR STORY

WALL STREET
The Story of the Stock Market

ELLEN'S BLUE JAYS

by Dorothy and Philip Sterling

POLIO PIONEERS

Forever Free

The story of the
Emancipation Proclamation

by Dorothy Sterling

Illustrated by Ernest Crichlow

DOUBLEDAY & COMPANY, INC., GARDEN CITY, NEW YORK

I SHOULD LIKE TO THANK MR. BENJAMIN A. BOTKIN AND THE UNIVERSITY OF CHICAGO PRESS FOR PERMISSION TO REPRINT THE EXCERPTS FROM SLAVES' STORIES WHICH APPEAR ON PAGES 94, 95–96, 117 and 118. THESE NARRATIVES WERE ORIGINALLY PUBLISHED IN MR. BOTKIN'S *Lay My Burden Down*, COPYRIGHT 1946 BY THE UNIVERSITY OF CHICAGO.

Contents

Contents

Forever Free

THE STORY OF THE
EMANCIPATION PROCLAMATION

The Day of Jubilee

We had a grand time at Boston, on the first of January. . . . We all seemed to be about of one color that day.

—FREDERICK DOUGLASS

THE promise was made in September, the second September of the war. The President wrote it out in the formal language of government for all the world to read. A preliminary Emancipation Proclamation. If the Southern states continued in their rebellion against the United States, then on January 1, 1863, their slaves would be declared free.

There were four million slaves in the South. One eighth of the country's entire population was in bondage. Now the President was promising them freedom in one hundred days. It wasn't a long time to wait for men and women who had waited two hundred and fifty years. But it was long enough.

They brought in the corn from the fields. They

hung the floppy tobacco leaves in the sheds and the hams in the smokehouses. They picked the bursting bolls of cotton.

Pumpkins ripened on the vines. Scarlet and gold leaves dropped from the trees. Birds winged their way to sunny Southern hedgerows. Men died in battle. Slaves, listening to the promise on the grapevine telegraph, flocked to the Union lines.

The long, anxious days dragged on. Eighty more days, sixty.

"Mr. President, they say you are not going to keep your promise to give us the Emancipation Proclamation, that it is your intention to withdraw it."

"Mr. President, the Proclamation is fraught with evil, and evil only."

"Mr. President, I have a petition here . . . Mr. President, I represent five hundred men in my district . . ."

Forty days, twenty days. Would he do it? Dare he?

Ten days. "The border state pressure on the President to withdraw the Emancipation Proclamation grows intense," the Cincinnati *Gazette* informed its readers.

Nine days. "There is reason both for hope and fear," Frederick Douglass, newspaper editor and former slave, wrote. "Alas, no man can tell which will prevail—and we are compelled to wait, hope, labor and pray."

Four days. "You will be glad to know that the President is firm," Senator Charles Sumner assured a friend.

The President is weak. The President is firm. As clocks ticked off the final hours, the rumors spread, the pressures mounted, the prayers grew louder.

On New Year's Eve churches in every city in the North held Watch Night services. "I don't want anyone to pray standing up," a Washington minister warned his congregation. "Nobody sitting down, with bended neck praying; and no brother kneeling on one knee, because his pants are too tight for him. Get down *on both knees* to thank Almighty God for your freedom, and President Lincoln too."

When city bells rang at midnight men and women jumped to their feet to shout, to kiss, to sing, "What a Happy New Year." At last the hundred days were at an end.

But what would the hundred and first day bring?

Snow and rain drove the celebrators from the streets. All along the Atlantic seaboard early risers faced a bleak dawn. Bundling up in shawls and scarves, they tramped through slush to the newspaper offices. No news yet of the President's Proclamation. Some said that the announcement would be made at noon. Others, looking at the overcast sky, predicted that it would never come at all.

Despite the uncertainty, friends of freedom went ahead with their plans to celebrate the day. Down in South Carolina where the Union Army held a narrow strip of coast, soldiers and ex-slaves joined forces for a barbecue. In Norfolk, Virginia, five thousand newly freed men paraded through the streets to the home of the military governor. From Maine to Michigan people were crowding into churches and meeting halls.

In Boston the Music Hall filled up early for a grand jubilee concert. Everyone who was anyone in literary New England was there—Henry Wadsworth Long-fellow, John Greenleaf Whittier, Oliver Wendell Holmes. As they waited for the orchestra to tune up, Ralph Waldo Emerson climbed up to the stage to read "a string of verses, a sort of Boston hymn" that he had written that morning.

Hearts beat faster and gloved hands clapped as he read:

> "I break your bonds and masterships
> And I unchain the slave:
> Free be his heart and hand henceforth
> As wind and wandering wave."

Then came the music. It was a program carefully chosen to suit the joyful occasion: Beethoven's Fifth Symphony, Handel's Hallelujah Chorus, Mendelssohn's Hymn of Praise.

"Watchman, will the night soon pass?" a wailing voice sang.

"The night is departing. The day is approaching," the grand chorus boomed the answer.

But was there cause for joy? People were beginning to stir uneasily, to look questioningly around the auditorium. Noon had come and gone. The afternoon shadows were lengthening—and there was still no news from the White House.

In Tremont Temple, a few squares away, Frederick Douglass and other Negro and white abolitionists had been meeting since morning. As speaker followed speaker to the platform, the audience grew restless. "It wasn't logic," Douglass said, "but the trump of jubilee which everybody wanted to hear."

Would they hear it?

At seven lanterns were lit and someone carried a giant candle to the speakers' table. Outside, messengers lined the streets between the telegraph office and the Temple, stamping their feet in the snow and swinging their arms in order to keep warm. They waited—hopefully, fearfully.

Eight o'clock, nine o'clock. By ten the crowded hall was plunged in gloom and the speakers sounded less confident. What was happening in Washington? Would word never come?

There was only one man who knew the answer. He rose early that New Year's morning to sit in his office on the second floor of the White House. The whole country had offered him advice. Some of it he had taken. All of it he had listened to patiently. Now he alone had to decide.

He chewed on the wooden tip of his pen as he looked over the changes in the Proclamation that Cabinet members had suggested a day earlier. Then, taking a clean sheet of paper from his desk, he started to write.

"I, Abraham Lincoln, President of the United States . . ."

Before he had finished, servants on the floor below were arranging chairs and setting out bowls of punch and eggnog in the East Room. He scarcely had time to dress before the first of the New Year's Day callers arrived—beribboned diplomats, bonneted society matrons, booted generals, congressmen from the West who looked as awkward as the President in their rusty black tail coats.

For the next hours the tall man greeted an endless procession of visitors, stooping to shake hands, bowing to the ladies, smiling his tired smile. He heard nothing but "Happy New Year," "How do you do?" said nothing but "The same to you, ma'am," "Thank you for your kind wishes."

Late in the afternoon, when the last caller had taken his leave, Secretary of State Seward climbed the White House stairs. In his hand he carried the paper that Lincoln had written that morning. It was an official document now, with the great seal of the United States properly affixed. All that it needed was the President's signature.

Lincoln laid it on his desk and reached for his pen. Pen in mid-air, he hesitated.

"I never in my life felt more certain that I was doing right than I do in signing this paper," he told Seward. "But I have been shaking hands since nine o'clock this morning, till my arm is stiff and numb. This signature is one that will be closely examined, and if they find my hand trembled they will say, 'He had some compunctions.' But"—he flexed his aching fingers—"it is going to be done."

Dipping his pen in the inkstand, wiping it carefully so that no blot would mar the page, he slowly wrote *Abraham Lincoln* at the bottom of the Emancipation Proclamation.

Eight o'clock, nine o'clock, ten. Suddenly a man in formal clothes walked across the stage of the Music Hall. A breathless messenger pushed his way down the crowded aisle of Tremont Temple.

"It's coming! Over the wires—it's coming over the wires—now!"

The Music Hall audience sprang to its feet, waving hats and handkerchiefs. Dignified men whooped and ladies who had never before raised their voices joined in giving three mighty cheers, and three more, and three again, for President Lincoln. Pioneer abolitionist William Lloyd Garrison and Harriet Beecher Stowe, author of *Uncle Tom's Cabin,* were spotted in the gallery. Mrs. Stowe stood up—"the little woman who started this great war," Lincoln had called her —her bonnet crooked, her eyes damp. The roar of applause could be heard all the way to Boston Common.

At Tremont Temple the scene was even wilder. Tears mingled with cheers, sobs with shouts of praise. All speeches stopped, all voices joined in song:

"Sound the loud timbrel o'er Egypt's dark sea,
Jehovah hath triumphed, his people are free."

When the room quieted, a member of the Massachusetts legislature read the President's message.

"'Whereas, on the twenty-second day of September, in the year of our Lord one thousand eight hundred and sixty-two, a proclamation was issued by the President of the United States, containing, among other things, the following, to wit:

"'That on the first day of January, in the year of our Lord one thousand eight hundred and sixty-three, all persons held as slaves within any State, or designated part of a State, the people whereof shall then be in rebellion against the United States, shall be then, thenceforward and forever free. . . .'"

"Forever free!" A woman sitting in the front row crooned the phrase.

Smiling down at her, the speaker went on.

"'Now, therefore I, Abraham Lincoln, President of the United States, by virtue of the power in me vested as commander-in-chief of the army and navy of the United States in time of actual armed rebellion against authority and government of the United States, and as a fit and necessary war measure for suppressing said rebellion, do, on this first day of January, in the year of our Lord one thousand eight hundred and sixty-three . . . order and declare that all persons held as slaves within said designated States, and parts of States are and henceforward shall be free. . . .

"'And I hereby enjoin upon the people so declared to be free to abstain from all violence, unless in necessary self-defense; and I recommend to them that, in all cases when allowed, they labor faithfully for reasonable wages.

"'And I further declare and make known that such persons of suitable condition will be received into the armed service of the United States, to garrison forts, positions, stations, and other places, and to man vessels of all sorts in said service.

"'And upon this act, sincerely believed to be an act of justice warranted by the Constitution upon military necessity, I invoke the considerate judgment of mankind and the gracious favor of Almighty God. . . .'"

There was a storm of cheers and "Amens." Frederick Douglass stepped to the front of the platform to lead the audience in another hymn:

"Blow ye the trumpet, blow
The gladly solemn sound;
Let all the nations know,
To earth's remotest bound,
The year of jubilee is come!"

With tear-stained cheeks, men and women jammed the aisle, hugging friend and stranger. When Tremont Temple closed at midnight no one wanted to go home. They tramped through the frosty streets to the Twelfth Baptist Church, packing the small building from doors to pulpit. "We got into such a state of enthusiasm," Douglass said, "that almost everything

seemed to be witty and appropriate." The first rays of
sun were streaking Boston Harbor when the rejoic-
ing came to an end.

Forever Free. One-hundred-gun salutes greeted the
news in Washington, Pittsburgh, Buffalo, New York.
In Salem the artillery paraded across the Common.
At Dartmouth College students rang the chapel bell,
tugging at the rope for three joyful hours.

"A beautiful day," Henry Wadsworth Longfellow
wrote in his diary. "A day for poetry and song, a new
song," Frederick Douglass said.

The Beginning

Speaking of dragon's teeth, I think they were sown when the first cargo of Negroes were brought into Jamestown. You believe in Providence—will you tell me why He allowed the African to be made a slave in this country?

—Abraham Lincoln

The new day and its new song slowly traveled through the South.

"A Yankee soldier told someone in Williamsburg that Marse Lincoln done signed the 'Mancipation. Was winter time and mighty cold that night, but everybody commence gettin' ready to leave. Didn't care nothin' 'bout Missus—was goin' to the Union lines. An' all that night the Negroes danced an' sang right out in the cold. Next mornin' at day-break we all started out with blankets an' clothes an' pots an' pans an' chickens piled on our backs. An' as the sun come up over the trees the Negroes all started to singin'."

"Them Freedom Days! Never was no time like 'em

before or since. Negroes shoutin' and clappin' hands
and singin'! Children runnin' all over the place beatin'
tins and yellin'. Everybody happy. Sure did some cel-
ebratin'. Run to the kitchen and shout in the window:

> "Mammy, don't you cook no mo'.
> You's free! You's free!

Run to the henhouse an' shout:

> "Rooster, don't you crow no mo'.
> You's free! You's free!

Go to the pigpen an' tell the pig:

> "Ol' pig, don't you grunt no mo'.
> You's free! You's free!

Tell the cows:

> "Ol' cow, don't you give no mo' milk.
> You's free! You's free!

An' some smart alec boys sneaked up under Miss Sara
Ann's window and shouted:

> "Ain't got to slave no mo'.
> We's free! We's free!"

Wherever the Union Army marched, "shouting the
battle cry of freedom," slaves dropped their hoes and
rushed to join it. Even before the Emancipation Proclamation was signed slaves had been swarming to
Fortress Monroe at Old Point Comfort in Virginia.

They drifted down the James River on rafts, using
faded flannel blankets for sails. They crossed Chesapeake Bay at night in "borrowed" oyster boats or they

paddled up to the gates of the high-walled brick fortress in hollowed-out log canoes.

So many thousands came that Fortress Monroe was known as "the Freedom Fort."

The Freedom Fort at Old Point Comfort. If the slaves, paddling eagerly toward liberty in their home-made boats, had searched the length and breadth of the continent they could not have found a more dramatic spot at which to land. For it was here, on this peninsula at the mouth of the James River, that their long bondage had begun.

The year was 1619, sixteen months before the *Mayflower* dropped anchor in Plymouth Harbor. John Rolfe, onetime husband of Pocahontas and secretary of the Virginia Company, told the story:

"About the latter end of August, a Dutch man of Warr of the burden of a 160 tons arrived at Point Comfort, the commanders name Capt. Jope, his pilott for the West Indyes, one Mr. Marmaduke an Englishman. He brought not anything but 20 and odd Negars which the Governor and Cape Marchant bought for victualle at the best and easiest rates they could."

A Dutch ship with an Englishman for a pilot had been cruising in West Indian waters. The Dutch had captured a Spanish frigate with a load of Africans in its hold. In the best piratical tradition of the time, they had hijacked the Spaniards' cargo. As they sailed up the North American coast they were beset by storms. When their food and water ran low they put in at Jamestown to trade their booty for venison and Indian corn.

The Virginia colonists welcomed them. Many of the settlers were impoverished gentlemen, younger sons of dukes and lords whose hands grew blistered when they grasped an ax or hoe. They were glad to buy the sturdy, dark-skinned prisoners, no questions asked, "at the best and easiest rates."

Only the Africans saw anything wrong in the transaction.

The Emancipation Proclamation had its beginnings on that fateful August day in 1619 when twenty men and women huddled on the beach at Point Comfort. Antonio, Pedro, Angelo, Isabella, Michaela—for their Spanish captors had renamed them—were the first to come in chains.

Others followed. A score, twoscore Africans trickled into the colony in succeeding years. By 1650 three hundred Negroes were working on the plantations of Virginia. Antonio became Anthony, Pedro Peter, and their children answered to the good English names of William, Mary, John.

Up and down the Atlantic coast the trickle slowly became a stream. In 1626 the Dutch West India Company brought eleven Negroes to New Amsterdam. In 1639 a Salem sea captain unloaded a cargo of salt, tobacco, and black men on the wharf at Boston. In 1670 Carolina's proprietors planted their first settlement at Charleston with the help of a trio of Africans.

By the end of the century the stream was a swelling tide. Twenty-five thousand unwilling immigrants were being carried to the New World each year. Wherever there were settlers, there were slaves. Wherever there were slaves, the long struggle for freedom was under way.

Before the Beginning

Savages we call them because their manners differ from ours, which we think the perfection of civility. They think the same of theirs.
—BENJAMIN FRANKLIN

FIFTY years before Columbus crossed the Atlantic, Portuguese and Spanish sailors explored the west coast of Africa. As traders followed the explorers, Europeans caught a glimpse of the riches of the Dark Continent. Peanuts and palm oil, ivory and gold—and men.

The first Africans brought to Europe were curiosities. People came to see them almost as if they were animals in a zoo. Princes and noblemen bid against each other for the possession of a dark-skinned page boy or a dusky handmaiden.

No one knew what to call these strange exotic creatures. The Spanish spoke of them as *Negros* after their word for "black." The English referred to them as "blackamoors" or "Ethiopians." In the freewheeling spelling of those days, the words might be written as "Negars," "blackamores," "Aethiops," or simply "Moors."

To the men and women of Europe, all of the Africans seemed alike. They were heathens, naked savages—cannibals, perhaps—and they lacked the advantages of the Christian religion and European culture and know-how.

Had the Europeans looked more closely they would have seen that their captives were not alike, even in appearance. The Africans were tall, short, middling. Their hair was closely curled or straight, their noses narrow or broad. The color of their skins ranged from yellow-brown and copper to chocolate and to a deep black that was almost purple. They looked no more alike than the tall blond Swedes of the North Sea and the short, swarthy Italians who lived along the shores of the Mediterranean.

The Negroes of Africa were not one people but many. They spoke different languages, had different customs and long, proud histories. Some lived in jungle villages, raising rice and millet, cotton and wheat, or tending herds of cows, goats, and sheep. Others lived in cities with palm-lined streets, busy market places, and stone palaces for their kings.

Leo Africanus, an African slave brought to the court of Pope Leo X, described the kingdom of Songhay (now the Republic of Mali) around the time of Columbus.

"Corne, cattle, milke, and butter this region yeeldeth in great abundance: but salt is verie scarce here. I saw one camels loade of salt sold for 80 ducates. The rich king of Timbuktu hath many plates and sceptres of gold, and he keepes a magnificent and well-furnished court. Here are great store of doctors, judges, priests and other learned men, that are bountifully maintained at the kings cost and charges. And hither are brought divers manuscripts or written books out of Barbary, which are sold for more money than any other merchandise."

Naked savages? Hardly. African climate didn't permit the silk knee breeches, brocaded gowns, and foothigh hairdresses that were the mark of their civilized captors. But they wore robes draped over one shoulder in the manner of Roman togas, or smocks and headcloths that were brilliant in color and pattern.

Wherever they lived, whatever they wore, these dark-skinned peoples were craftsmen. When Europeans were still dwelling in caves and using crude stone tools, African blacksmiths knew how to smelt iron over charcoal fires and forge knives and axes that were ornamental as well as useful. Long before the time of Columbus, Africans wove cotton and linen cloth and a remarkable rich velvet made from the leaves of banana plants. Later workmen carved ivory and wood in intricate designs and fashioned the beautiful bronzes of Benin which are now in museums all over the world.

The Europeans were correct about one thing, however. The Africans were not Christians. Some were Mohammedans, turning their faces toward Mecca to pray, but most worshiped many gods, the sky god, the earth god, the moon, as well as the spirits of their ancestors. Clearly it was the duty of the Portuguese and Spanish to convert them to Christianity—by making them slaves.

Actually the holy war that Europe waged against Africa was only a halfhearted one. It might have come to an end in the sixteenth century if it had not been for the discovery and settlement of America. As the plantations of the West Indies and the colonies on the mainland increased in size and importance there was an enormous need for labor. Cheap, steady labor to clear the forests, build the houses, plant the fields.

The Indians wouldn't do. The colonists tried them first, but they died of white men's diseases, refused to work, ran away. Nor were the poor of Europe the answer to the problem. In the same year that "twenty Negars" landed in Virginia, one hundred homeless children were sent there from London to serve as indentured servants until they were twenty-five. English prisons were raided, men and women kidnaped from the streets, children spirited away from their parents. But there were not enough homeless, helpless people in all of Europe to do the work that needed to be done.

That left the Africans.

To fill the huge demand for labor, a new kind of business enterprise came into being—the slave trade. Traders built settlements along a 5000-mile expanse of shore, from the Senegal River in the north to the mouth of the Congo, below the equator. These settlements were called factories. At the heart of each factory was a massive stone castle with slitted windows for gun emplacements, barracks for soldiers, offices for bookkeepers and clerks. In the shadow of the castles' guns stood warehouses for the storage of trading goods and pens, known as barracoons, where the slaves were herded before shipment.

People of almost every country in Europe took part in the slave trade—the Portuguese, the Dutch, French, Swedes, Danes, Germans. But the English and their cousins in New England gradually became its masters.

Shipbuilding boomed along the Thames. New industries sprang up in Manchester and Birmingham to manufacture the goods needed for trading: cheap calicoes, bright-colored beads, brass pans, rum, and gunpowder. In Liverpool, waterfront shops displayed an ingenious instrument known as a *speculum oris,* used to pry open the closed jaws of Africans who preferred starvation to slavery. To say nothing of leg shackles, handcuffs, thumbscrews, and cat-o'-nine-tails, which were standard tools of the trade.

Some Africans became businessmen too. Natives along the coast whose spears had been shattered by the white men's guns recognized an old saying: If you can't lick 'em, join 'em. They delivered captives to the barracoons and were given cotton cloth and brass pans and rum in payment. Lacking the advan-

tages of European culture and knowhow, they seldom
grew rich, however. The cloth they received was far
inferior to the product of local weavers and as for the
rum . . . A Rhode Island merchant wrote to the
captain of his ship: "Make yr Cheaf Trade with the
Blacks. Worter yr Rum as much as possible and sell
as much by the short mesuer as you can."

Africa had known slavery before the white men
came. Prisoners captured in battle were enslaved. So
were men who had shown disrespect to their rulers,
or women suspected of witchcraft, or debtors forced
to work off their debts. The slaves, like those in
Greece a thousand years earlier, were usually well
treated. Sometimes they married their captors'
daughters or won their freedom after years in bondage.

But Africa had never known modern slavery. Prisoners of war, debtors, witches couldn't begin to fill
the ships that dropped anchor off Cape Coast Castle
and Fort Louis and Castle Christianborg. Manstealing
had to take place on a large scale. Whole villages
were kidnaped, whole cities wiped out of existence.
And the slaves could no longer hope to marry their
captors' daughters or win freedom someday.

Modern slavery was different. It was a big business, the biggest business in the world before it was
over. Operating between the continents of Europe,
Africa, and the New World, it was efficiently organized, immensely profitable—and unspeakably brutal.

A Story

I asked "What had induced them to mutiny?" They answered "I was a great Rogue to buy them, in order to carry them away from their own Country, and that they were resolved to regain their liberty."
—CAPTAIN WILLIAM SNELGRAVE, 1754

KAMBA—his name could have been Kisimi, Kai-Kai, Ibrahim—was in the rice field, half a league from the village.

"Eiye! Eiye!" He ran between the rows, shouting and waving his arms. It was his job to scare the birds away from the ripening grain.

"Eiye——" A hand was clamped over his mouth. His wrists were tied behind his back and he found himself on the path that led to the river.

"Eiye!" Kamba tried to shout again, but only the birds, circling overhead, could hear him. Then it was quiet in the field. The birds slowly dropped to the ground to feast undisturbed on the plump kernels of grain.

Kamba stumbled on, heart thumping loudly, eyes blinded by tears. Along the riverbank, past the spot where he bathed each morning, farther and farther away from the village. Downstream, hidden at first by a clump of cottonwood trees, a crowd of people had gathered. Some were strange beings with light hair and pale faces and guns. Others were captives, boys like himself, women with babies on their backs, grown men.

Soon Kamba found himself lying in the bottom of a canoe with another boy almost on top of him. Hours passed. As the canoe slid through the water, all Kamba could see was the sky. Once it rained, a torrential African rain, and he closed eyes and mouth, gasping for breath. With the dusk, mosquitoes came. He struggled to free his hands so that he could slap them, but the tough grass rope only cut into his wrists. Kamba, twelve years old and big for his age, lay in the water-soaked canoe and cried.

All that night they traveled downstream, farther and farther away from home. Kamba cried and prayed and thought about his mother. In the morning he was done with crying.

The boy above him, talking in a dialect that Kamba could barely understand, said that they were headed for the ocean. Kamba had heard about the ocean, many days away. His father had once made a trading trip there, selling casks of palm oil and returning to the village with salt. His father had returned home safely. Perhaps he could too.

At midday the canoes pulled over to shore and the captives were ordered to get out. Kamba slowly climbed up the bank, shoulders stiff, legs aching, wrists sore. His blue smock was dripping wet and he shook himself as if he were a dog at a water hole.

Someone untied his hands and motioned him toward a large iron pot filled with beans. Kamba ate carefully, picking up the beans between thumb and forefinger, as his mother had taught him to. In spite of the lump that kept rising in his throat he was hungry.

When the meal was over he looked longingly at the gray-green river, wishing he could bathe and feel clean. But there was no time for baths.

"Up!" Guards ordered them to their feet, tying them together, neck to neck, with a long strap of leather. A man who tried to run away had chains fastened to his ankles—not grass rope, but heavy iron chains that clanked when he walked. Turning their backs on the river, they marched single file on a narrow twisting path through the jungle.

The sun rose and set, but Kamba lost all track of time. His feet were blistered, his muddy arms scratched, and the leather thong pressed against his windpipe. In front of him, a woman stumbled and fell. Guards lashed her with their whips. When she failed to rise they cut her out of the line and marched on.

A day, a night, a day of walking. Then the trees thinned out and Kamba could see through them to a stretch of sandy beach. Gray rocks, yellow beach, blue water—endless blue water, just as his father had described it. But there was a huge white fortress on the rocks, armed men on the sand, and ships a hundred times as big as any African canoe rocking on the blue water.

In the slave pen on the beach they took away his tattered smock and left him to lie naked, his ankle tied to a post driven into the sand. Kamba thought of the village sheep, tethered to bushes at the edge of the clearing so that they wouldn't stray. In the morning he was reminded of the sheep again. Guards shaved his head, scrubbed him down with wet sand, and rubbed him with palm oil until his skin shone. It was like market day at home when the sheep and the pigs were made ready for sale.

After the baths were over a white man entered the barracoon. Everyone was ordered to jump up and down while he listened to noises in their chests, looked at their teeth, and prodded and poked all parts of their bodies. Kamba seemed to have passed this test, for then, two guards held him face down in the sand while a third pressed a searing-hot iron between his shoulder blades. Tethered, shorn, branded as if he were a yearling lamb, Kamba was now a part of the white man's herd.

The branding over, he listened to the rumors that flew around the barracoon. . . . Tonight, tomorrow for sure, we are going to be sacrificed to the white men's gods or sent far across the sea. . . . With the blazing sun beating down on his bare body, Kamba shivered.

What could he do? He knew how to braid grass rope into mats for the floor of his mother's hut, how to chase the birds and mind the sheep and climb the tall palm trees when the coconuts were ripe. He knew the stories of his gods and the songs of his people and he was learning the complicated language of the talking drum which carried messages to the villages up and down the river. If only he had a drum now so that he could call for help. Then his father and his uncles and the brave men of his tribe would come to rescue him.

But this was a dream and twelve-year-old Kamba knew that it would not come true. His chin sank down on his chest and he stretched his arm over his shoulder, feeling the sore place where the white man's brand had blistered his skin. There was nothing he could do against the whips and guns of the guards. No one could hear his call for help.

Another long day passed. Looking over the mud wall of the barracoon, Kamba watched a fleet of canoes putting out for the squat black schooner offshore. First, casks and barrels, the supplies for the voyage, were loaded. Then it was time for the human cargo.

Men, women, children, they were lined up at the gate of the barracoon, the men and older boys chained together with iron collars that snapped around their necks. Still naked, except for the rusty

links of chain, they marched to the shore. Before they
stepped into the canoes a priest sprinkled sand over
their shaven heads and chanted a prayer to keep the
evil spirits away.

It was Kamba's last word from Africa.

As the canoes cut through the choppy surf two
women leaped over the side. One was torn to pieces
by a shark before the guards could get to her. Kamba
closed his eyes so that he wouldn't see the streaks
of red in the blue water.

"Better to look," the man next to him said. "And
remember."

In the next days Kamba looked, but there were
things he tried not to remember. Placed in the hold
with the men, he had to lie on his side, with his
nose pressed against his neighbor's back. "Not so
much space as a man in a coffin," someone grunted.

In fair weather the portholes were left open, but
when a storm threatened a sailor crawled over their
sweating bodies to close them. Then the hot stale air
was overpowering. Many fainted. Many came down
with dread diseases—plague and dysentery and a
sickness of the eyes called ophthalmia. Many died.

In the mornings, weather permitting, they were allowed up on deck. Their chains were removed and
Kamba turned his head and flexed his legs and swung
his arms around. Even breathing had become a special treat.

They were fed in groups of ten, arranged in a cir-
cle around a wooden tub. Some mornings Kamba

was too seasick to eat. On others, he plunged both hands into the tub, his table manners all but forgotten.

After the meal was over they were ordered to exercise. While one prisoner kept time by thumping on the bottom of an empty tub, the others went through the motions of a joyless dance. A sailor with a cat-o'-nine-tails brought it down on the bare back of anyone who was slow to join in.

On their second day at sea, when the African coast was still a faint dark line on the horizon, there was a sudden scuffle on deck. Before Kamba understood what was happening, a tall slave had attacked the captain with a chunk of iron torn from the forecastle door. One of his companions wrestled with the mate, forcing him toward the rail, while others struck at the sailors with their food tubs.

For a few minutes the ship was in an uproar. A sailor and a slave went overboard, still locked in angry embrace when the sharks caught up with them. Then the mutiny was over. Men, no matter how desperate, could not fight barehanded for long against guns and cutlasses.

During the rest of the trip they were kept in leg shackles, day and night. While they ate, members of the crew stood on guard with loaded guns. When they danced, the rattling of their chains added a curious mournful note to the music of the upturned tub.

Although there were no more mutinies, the struggle between captive and captor still continued.

Women with babies in their arms threw themselves over the side of the ship to dance triumphantly on the waves until they disappeared from view. Men sat in front of the tubs of food with folded arms and lips firmly closed, refusing to eat. If they were fed forcibly, they had still another way to resist. They simply stopped breathing, holding their breaths until they toppled onto the deck. The sharks Kamba had seen in African waters followed the schooner across the Atlantic. They did not lack for food.

For days at a time, when gale winds rocked the ship, Kamba lay on his side in the stifling hold, listening to the screams of men who had lost their minds, to the shouts of the defiant ones and the moans of the dying. The voyage lasted two months and eleven days. One hundred and ninety-two men and women out of a cargo of four hundred died during the trip.

Kamba lived.

He was thin, with bony elbows and knobby knees, when he planted his feet on dry land again. He had sores on his ankles where the chains had rubbed them, and a brand between his shoulder blades. He was cut off from his past and he had no notion of what the future held in store for him.

But he was alive and with life there was hope.

Of Horses and Men

Captain Ball was a Yankee slaver,
Blow, blow, blow the man down!
He traded in Negroes and loved
his Saviour,
Give me some time to blow the
man down.

—Old Sea Chanty

Kamba's story is no different from the story of millions of Africans who were kidnaped from their homes and sold into slavery in the lands across the sea. The horrors of the middle passage between Africa and the Americas have been described by innumerable eyewitnesses:

Complaint of a ship's captain, 1693: "The Negroes are so wilful and loth to leave their own country that they have often leap'd out of the canoos, boat and ship, into the sea, and kept under water till they were drowned."

Account by a ship's doctor, 1788: "I have seen coals of fire, glowing hot, put on a shovel and placed so near their lips as to scorch and burn them, with threats of forcing them to swallow the coals if they persisted in refusing to eat."

Report to the House of Lords, 1789: "It was the business of the chief mate to make the men dance and the second mate danced the women; but this was only done by means of a frequent use of the cat. The men could only jump up and rattle their chains."

Testimony before a committee of the House of Commons, 1791: "The Negroes were chained to each other hand and foot, and stowed so close that they were not allowed above a foot and a half for each in breadth. Thus rammed together like herrings in a barrel, they contracted putrid and fatal disorders."

Diary of a twelve-year-old boy traveling from Africa to Guadeloupe, 1819: "The Captain is in the best temper in the world; he walks the deck, rubbing his hands and humming a tune. He says he has six dozen slaves on board, men, women and children, and all in prime marketable condition. I have not seen them, however, since we set sail. Their cries are so terrible that I do not like to go and look down in the hold. . . .

"Today, word was brot to the Captain that two of the slaves were dead, suffocated, as was supposed, by the closeness of the hold; and he immediately ordered the rest should be brot up to the forecastle to give them air. . . .

"They had no sooner reached the ship's side than first one, then another, then a third, sprang up on the gunwale and darted into the sea. Many more made the attempt, but without success; they were all knocked flat to the deck and the crew kept watch over them with handspikes and cutlasses. . . .

"When the Captain came up on deck and was told of the revolt, his face grew pale, and he gnashed his teeth. 'We must make an example' said he. He then ordered the whole of the slaves in the ship to be tied together, and having selected six, he caused three of them to be shot, and the other three hanged, before the eyes of their comrades.

"Last night I could not sleep. I thot the six Negroes were passing to and fro through the cabin and looking in at the door of the Captain's stateroom. At last I began to pray so loud that I awoke him, and he asked me, what was the matter. 'I am saying my prayers,' said I. 'That is a good boy,' replied he, and in an instant he was as sound asleep as before."

Fifteen million Africans were transported to America in the years between 1492 and 1863. Perhaps an equal number perished on the way, their bones bleaching on the paths through the jungle, or their flesh devoured by sharks. These were not the weaklings of African society, but the youngest, the strongest, the most able. With their departure civilization over a large part of the continent was set back for centuries. Yet the leaders of the slave trade were not criminals but respected gentlemen.

John Hawkins, the first Englishman of note to sail to Africa, was famous for his piety. His crew was in-

structed to "serve God daily" and to "love one
another" while they chained men to the decks of the
good ships *Jesus, Angel,* and *Grace of God.* Hawkins
carefully selected his victims, preferring the natives
of the Cape Verde Islands, "of a nature very gentle
and loving," to their more rebellious neighbors on the
mainland. Queen Elizabeth was one of Hawkins'
backers. When she knighted him for his services he
chose a coat of arms consisting of "a demi-Moor
bound and captive."

Hawkins was followed by the Company of Royal
Adventurers of England Trading to Africa—a company that included members of the royal family,
three dukes, eight earls, seven lords, and twenty-
seven knights! Later, royalty shared the business with
middle-class merchants who were leaders in their
communities and pillars of their church.

How could these men turn from their Bibles to
read the bloody records of the slave trade? How
could they sleep at night with the knowledge of
wholesale kidnapings and mass murders on their
consciences?

Part of the answer lay in the enormous profits of
the business. A slave purchased for fifty dollars in
Africa could be sold in America for four hundred.
The slave trade not only lined the pockets of
individual merchants. Its demand for ships and trading goods made it one of the mainstays of British industry and New England commerce.

"Tho' to traffic in human creatures, may at first

sight appear barbarous, inhuman, and unnatural, from this trade proceed benefits far outweighing all real or pretended mischiefs and inconveniences," one merchant said.

"The slave trade is certainly not an amiable trade," another agreed. "Neither is that of a butcher. Yet it is a very necessary one."

The slave trade was profitable. The slave trade was necessary. Still one more excuse was needed to put uneasy consciences at rest.

In 1783 the captain of the *Zong* threw one hundred and thirty-two slaves into the sea when his supply of water ran low. An English judge ruled that he was entitled to insurance money for the men and women he had drowned because "The case of slaves was the same as if horses had been thrown overboard."

The judge had found the best excuse of all. The dark-skinned people of Africa were different from Europeans. They were something less than human. Therefore they could be treated as if they were horses or cows and no one had to worry about the teachings of Christ and the Golden Rule.

Charles Montesquieu, a French philosopher, was one of the few men of his time to speak against the slave trade. He summed up this excuse in a single bitter sentence:

"It would not do to suppose that Negroes were men, lest it should turn out that whites were not."

Making of an American

TWELVE-YEAR-OLD Kamba disembarked at Charleston, South Carolina, sometime around the year 1700. Still chained to his companions, he walked to the slave jail. The narrow streets seemed to pitch and roll and he had a hard time keeping his balance. Soon he was in a crowded room with high barred windows. A succession of white men barked commands. If only he could understand their strange clipped speech so that he could find out what was happening.

Dazed, frightened, he submitted numbly to a bath and a haircut. His chains were removed and he was given oil for his roughened skin and a bowl of steamy rice to put flesh back on his bony body. A white man tossed him a shirt and a pair of pants.

Kamba had to watch one of the other slaves dress before he knew what to do. Then he stepped into the pants, thrust his arms into the sleeves of the skirt, and awkwardly struggled to button them. They weren't as comfortable as his blue smock. The

pants rubbed against his sore ankles and the scratchy cloth of the shirt made his back itch. But after months of nakedness he was glad to be wearing clothes.

One morning the slaves were led from the jail to

a courtyard outside. Kamba blinked in the sunlight. A man turned him around, forcing his mouth open, pulling up his shirt. After grunting approvingly, he motioned Kamba to a wooden platform in the center of the yard.

Kamba looked down at a sea of strange white faces. Suddenly his legs trembled and tears filled his eyes.

The man who had examined his teeth began to frown. "Smile, boy, smile!" he commanded.

Kamba did his best to obey. He jumped up and down, hoping that he was following the white man's order. The tears rolled down his cheeks.

"*Smile!*" the white man shouted.

Kamba raised his hands above his head. Perhaps this was what the man wanted. Now he was really crying, sobbing as if he were a little boy back in his mother's hut.

Growing red with anger, the man lifted his arm threateningly.

"Smile." A Negro pushed his way through the crowd to talk to Kamba in his own language. "He wants you to look happy."

His body still racked by sobs, Kamba managed to turn up the corners of his mouth and flash his teeth. It was no more than a grimace, but it seemed to satisfy. After a brief discussion among the white men, a jerk of a thumb sent him to the corner of the yard. Along with other men and women from the ship, he had been sold to a rice planter.

They set out that afternoon, walking past Charleston's homes and gardens to a sandy road that led to the plantation. The land was fair. Blue skies, tall trees with shiny leaves, swampy meadows where many of the plants looked familiar. Every once in a while they passed a house, a big house painted white, with glass windows that reflected the long rays of the setting sun.

In spite of the rope around his neck, Kamba's spirits rose. It was good to walk after the long confinement of ship and jail. He practiced the word he'd learned, saying it silently and then out loud.

"Smile." Kamba had had his first English lesson.

There were many more lessons to be learned in the next months. A "salt-water Negro," he was put in a cabin with seasoned slaves whose job it was to break him in. There would be no more chasing birds away from the grain. From now on he must work like a man.

The overseer's horn awakened him each morning while it was still dark. On his way to the field he grabbed a handful of rice. By sunrise he was wading along the rows of plants, hoeing, weeding, reaping, binding. Sunset found him still stooping over, his back aching, his bare feet muddy and cold. After that there was supper to cook over the open fire in the cabin.

"We work from can to can't," one of the older slaves told him.

His first night on the plantation, Kamba couldn't

sleep. He played a little game, pretending that he was at home in the cone-shaped hut in which he had been born, that he was lying on a sweet-smelling grass mat instead of the bare dirt floor. His mother was singing a lullaby, or his father was telling a story in his deep grave voice. When morning came he would bathe in the cool water of the river and run after the emerald-green lizards that skittered over the rocks.

The second night he couldn't stay awake. As soon as his head touched the ground he sank into an exhausted sleep. His cabin mates had to shake him in the morning so that he would get to the field on time. Sometimes in those first weeks he slept standing up, his chin bobbing on his chest until the overseer's whip lashed him back to wakefulness.

As time passed he stopped playing the game about home. He forgot about his daily bath in the river, counting himself lucky if he had chance for one each week in a nearby stream. He forgot African sounds and smells. He could no longer picture his mother's face or recall his father's voice.

He even stopped praying to his gods. Those spirits of his ancestors who used to watch over him were clearly too far away to do any good. The sky god, the earth god, the moon god were here, but in this country they seemed to listen only to the white man.

Forgetting Africa, he learned America. He learned the ways of the plantation. How to work when the overseer was looking and rest on the hoe when his back was turned. How to get enough to eat by catching master's chickens or raiding master's vegetable patch in the dark of night.

"Stealing is a crime," the overseer warned. "Punishment, one hundred lashes on the bare back."

"Stealing's no crime," the Negroes whispered. "Less'n you steal from another slave. Or get caught. Eating master's chicken is just *taking*—taking out of one of master's pots and putting it in another."

He learned the strange harsh language of the white man. Single syllables at first: *eat, drink, sleep, work, whip, hoe, yes, no*. Then longer words: *master, mistress, overseer*—and *freedom*.

By the time Kamba had passed his thirteenth birthday his mother would scarcely have recognized him. He was still big for his age and growing bigger. His pants barely covered his knees and his muscled arms split the seams of his ragged shirt. He wasn't an African boy any more, or a salt-water greenhorn.

He was a Negro slave. His children, slave or free, would be Americans.

They Called Out Liberty

In dark fens of the Dismal Swamp
  The hunted Negro lay;
He saw the fire of the midnight camp,
And heard at times a horse's tramp
  And a bloodhound's distant bay.

Where hardly a human foot could pass,
  Or a human heart would dare,
On the quaking turf of the green morass
He crouched in the rank and tangled
                    grass,
  Like a wild beast in his lair.
                    —HENRY WADSWORTH LONGFELLOW

THE life of a slave in the years around 1700 varied according to where he lived and who owned him. If he was sold on the wharf in Boston or Newport he became a servant, working alongside mistress in the kitchen or sweeping floors and building fires in master's shop. In the Middle Colonies, he might work on a farm in the Hudson Valley, learning Dutch instead of English, or in the homes and counting rooms of Philadelphia and New York.

In Northern cities, slaves wore their owners' cast-off clothes, slept in the attics of their homes, and ate leftovers from their tables. Often they learned to

read and write so that they could become master's
clerk or messenger. Some Puritan masters read morning prayers to their slaves. In Quaker Pennsylvania
they were taught the Gospels and taken to meeting
on First Days.

Slavery was harsher in the South, where hundreds
of men and women worked side by side on the tobacco plantations and in Carolina's rice and indigo
fields. There, Negro and white lived apart, the
slaves in ramshackle cabins far from "the big houses."
Except for those who worked as servants, they had
little contact with their owners and less opportunity
for education than Northern slaves.

Yet, North or South, kind master or cruel one,
there was one subject on which all slaves agreed.
Whether he spoke Dutch, the cultivated accents of
Boston, or the pidgin English of a Carolina field
hand, every slave wanted to be free.

For the struggle that began on the slave ships
didn't end when Africans breathed the fresh air of
the New World. Fifty men and women waded into
shallow water off the Carolina coast and drowned
while their ship was tying up at the dock. Twelve
hanged themselves from the branches of a live oak
after they reached the plantation. A man threw himself into a stream when he was threatened with a
whipping. A woman smothered her newborn baby
so that he wouldn't grow up to be a slave.

In the religion of Africa, death meant a return to
the land of one's ancestors. Suicide, then, was one

way of going home. But as beliefs in African gods and memories of jungle villages began to fade, slaves turned away from self-destruction. Bitter and resentful, many sought revenge.

In 1695 a Connecticut slave put arsenic in his mistress' milk. A Boston girl blew up her master's house by dropping a burning coal into a keg of gunpowder. Two New Yorkers—a Negro woman and an Indian man—were burned at the stake for murdering master, mistress, and five children. Two Jersey slaves received similar punishment for burning seven Hackensack barns. White Virginians trembled when a series of fires broke out. Carolinians, living in "great fear and terror," complained of "the hellish practice of poisoning."

Desperate men who felt that they had nothing to lose banded together and fought for their freedom. Like the mutinies on the slave ships, the story of these revolts was almost always the same. An attack—a defeat—followed by swift and terrible punishment. Yet they continued year after year, for two long centuries.

Virginia, 1663. Slaves and white indentured servants were caught planning an uprising. Their ringleaders were drawn and quartered and their heads stuck up on posts in public places.

New York, 1712. Twenty-three slaves met at midnight in an orchard near the center of town. Early the next morning they set fire to a barn. As their masters approached, the slaves attacked with guns,

knives, hatchets. After nine citizens were killed the
governor ordered out a detachment of soldiers. When
the slaves were finally captured, "some were burnt,
others hanged, one broke on the wheele, and one
hung alive in chains. . . . There has been the most ex-
emplary punishment inflicted that could be possibly
thought of," the governor reported.

New Orleans, 1730. When a slave woman was
struck by a soldier she shouted angrily, "The French
shall not long insult Negroes." Because her shout
aroused suspicion, eight slaves, including one named
Samba, were arrested. "They were put to the torture
of burning matches; which, though several times re-
peated, could not bring them to make any confes-
sion," the director of plantations wrote. "In the
meantime I learnt that Samba had in his own country
been at the head of the revolt by which the French
lost Fort Arguin. On his passage he had laid a
scheme to murder the crew, in order to become master of the ship; but that being discovered, he was
put in irons." Samba and his companions were "broken
alive on the wheel," the slave woman hanged.

South Carolina, 1739. On a Sunday in September
a score of slaves fled from a plantation near Charleston. Attacking an arsenal, they killed the guards and
armed themselves with guns and powder. "Several
Negroes joyned them," an eyewitness wrote. "They
called out liberty, marched on with colours displayed and two drums beating. The Country there-
about was full of flames." Every white man along the

way was shot, except for an innkeeper who was "a good man and kind to his slaves."

They were eighty strong by the time the militia caught up with them. "An engagement ensued wherein one fought for Liberty & Life the other for their Country & everything that was Dear to them." Outnumbered, the slaves "fought stoutly for some time." Some were shot, "some hang'd, and some Gibbeted alive." Not all of them were captured however. "Some are out yet, but we hope will soon be taken," the lieutenant governor said. Months later, ten slaves were still "out." They were never returned to captivity.

In the first years of the eighteenth century the slaves in the South had one big advantage over their Northern brothers. Geography was on their side. In the populous colonies of New England and New York it was hard to find a place to hide. Runaways sometimes concealed themselves on ships or set out on foot for the distant wilderness of French-held Canada. In 1705 New York's General Assembly passed a law prohibiting slaves from "traveling 40 miles above the city of Albany, at or above a place called Sarachtoge (Saratoga) on pain of death."

In the South a slave could find freedom almost in his own back yard. Once he had passed the string of settlements along the coast, he had nothing in front of him but woods and swamp and stream. A slave could hide for years in the forests of the frontier where no white man had ever trod.

Many did.

From Great Dismal Swamp in Virginia to the Louisiana bayous and the Everglades of Florida, the dark, trackless places of the continent offered refuge to the brave. Some ran away for only a few weeks. One slave remembered how his mother "hid us all in the woods, to prevent master selling us. When we wanted water, she sought for it in any hole or puddle; it was often full of tadpoles and insects. She strained it and give it round to each of us in the hollow of her hand. For food, she gathered berries in the woods, got potatoes, raw corn, and so forth. After a time the master would send word to her to come in, promising he would not sell us."

Others remained in the swamps and glades all their lives. Great Dismal and its tributaries, Little Dismal, Alligator, and Catfish, covering a vast area in Virginia and North Carolina, sheltered thousands of fugitives. Children were born in the swamp, grew up there, bore children of their own, without ever catching a glimpse of the white world. They were called maroons, from the Spanish word *cimarrón,* meaning outlaw.

These black Robin Hoods lived off the countryside, hunting, fishing, trading with small farmers on the fringes of the swamp, stealing from outlying plantations and lumber camps. They stopped parties of horsemen who ventured into their territory and sallied forth occasionally to hold up country stores. In the back places they built huts, cleared land for planting, and raised cows and goats. One outlaw community, surprised by a group of South Carolinians, was described in a local newspaper:

"A trail, winding about much, conducted the party to a knoll in the swamp on which corn, squashes and peas were growing. Continuing the search, another patch of corn, etc. was found and a camp from which several Negroes fled. The camp seemed well provided with meal, cooking utensils, blankets."

Throughout their lives the maroons could never be free from fear. The snapping of a twig, a vine swaying on a windless day, a dog baying in the distance —any of these might mean ambush and attack. For there were prices on their heads, dead or alive, and hunters eager to win the rewards. Even Indians were sometimes persuaded to join the chase. An "Account of expenditures attending the dispersing the Fugitive Slaves near Purrysburg, South Carolina," tells of a payment of forty pounds to the Catawbas for scalps that they had taken.

Still men and women ran away to the woods. "Some of 'em would rather be shot than be took," a slave in Virginia said. Besides, not all of the danger was on one side. Colonists were often hesitant to track down fugitives who shared forest and mudhole with wildcats, snakes, and alligators. One Virginia deputy, armed with a warrant for the arrest of a runaway, trailed him through the tangled underbrush of Great Dismal. At last he sighted his quarry

—on the far side of a stretch of treacherous black waters. The deputy returned to the courthouse alone, to scratch a message across the face of his warrant: "See-able but not come-at-able."

Most of the accounts of maroon leaders are tantalizingly brief. The "General of the Swamps" led nighttime raids on North Carolina plantations. A Virginia store was held up "by a maroon banditti of Negroes" led by "the noted Andey, alias Billy James, better known by the name of Abellino."

Only occasionally there are descriptions of these men who, in another time and place, might have been hailed as heroes. Such a man was Joe, who took the name of Forest when he fled. "He was so cunning and artful as to elude pursuit and so daring and bold as to put everything at defiance," South Carolina planters complained. "Most of the runaways flew to his Camp and he soon became their head and their life. He had the art and the address to inspire enthusiasm. Such was his cunning that but few of the enterprises for mischief planned by himself failed of success. Nearly four years have now elapsed, the whole of which time was marked by Crimes, by Mischiefs and by the desemination of notions the most dangerous among the blacks in our Sections of the County (such as were calculated in the end to produce insubordination and insurrection)."

Several companies of infantry failed to dislodge Joe from his forest camp. He was trapped at last by the treachery of a fellow slave who led him into an ambush. "Soon perceiving their mistake, they instantly attempted to defend themselves with well-charged musquets but at a single well-directed fire from the party of whites Joe with three of his party fell dead. The rest of the gang of runaways were subsequently either killed in pursuit, hung for attempts to murder or were frightened to their respective homes."

As a reward for his cunning, the grateful state of South Carolina purchased Joe's betrayer and set him free.

Way Down upon the Suwanee River

Torn from their native land, they were sold in the markets of Carolina and Georgia . . . they fled to Florida, and under Spanish laws, became free. At a time of profound peace, our army . . . invaded Florida, murdered many of these free men, and brought others to the United States and consigned them to slavery. An expensive and bloody war followed.

—CONGRESSMAN JOSHUA R. GIDDINGS, 1858

THE most permanent of all the maroon camps were those in Florida. In the seventeenth and eighteenth centuries the Spanish governor welcomed fugitives from the English colonies and granted them freedom. The maroons built farming villages along the bottom lands of the Apalachicola and Suwanee rivers. They were joined by Indians who had broken away from the Creek tribe and were also seeking refuge. These Indians called themselves Seminoles, a word in their language which meant "runaways." For more than a hundred years the two groups of runaways—the red-skinned hunters and the black-skinned farmers—lived as allies, trading, intermarrying, and fighting side by side against a common foe.

The soil was rich, the climate warm, and the first maroon settlements flourished. Herds of cows grazed along the riverbanks, horses foraged in the woods, and the black farmers tilled their land in common as they had done in Africa. By the end of the eighteenth century the Florida maroons were scarcely entitled to their name, for they were living not as outlaws but as peaceful farmers and free men.

As the news of their prosperity traveled north across the border more and more slaves ran off to join them. From time to time Georgia and Carolina planters invaded the Spanish colony hunting for runaways. There was no serious trouble, however, until after the War of 1812. An English fleet anchored in Apalachicola Bay had sent troops upriver to build a fort in the heart of Negro farm country. When they withdrew at the end of the war they left the fort and its military stores in the hands of the maroons and Indians.

The Negroes continued to plow the soil and harvest their crops, happily unaware that they had become the subject of a series of dispatches between General Gaines, commander of the U. S. Army on Georgia's southern frontier, and the War Department in Washington. "Certain Negroes and outlaws have taken possession of a fort on the Apalachicola River, in the Territory of Florida," the general informed the Secretary of War. Throughout a year of correspondence about the "Negro Fort" and the "pirates" who occupied it, the maroons were never charged with crimes or hostile acts. It was sufficient that they were Negroes, descendants of slaves, cultivating the richest lands in Florida. Their very existence was a threat to Southern slaveowners and a standing invitation to runaways.

In spite of the fact that the Negro fort was sixty miles from the U.S. border, on land belonging to His Majesty the King of Spain, General Gaines was given a go-ahead signal from no less a person than General Andrew Jackson. "I have little doubt," Jackson wrote, "that this fort has been established by some villains for the purpose of rapine and plunder and that it ought to be blown up, regardless of the ground on which it stands; and if your mind shall have formed the same conclusion, destroy it and return the stolen Negroes and property to their rightful owners."

By midsummer of 1816 a full-scale expedition was under way. Two U.S. gunboats sailed up the Apalachicola River from the Gulf of Mexico while a regiment of soldiers, accompanied by five hundred Creeks, marched south from Georgia. Warned in plenty of time, the farmers along the river collected their families and fled to the fort for protection.

For days they held out against the cannonading. Shells whistled overhead, killing and wounding the refugees, but the strong fortress walls could not be breached. It wasn't until a freak shot struck the fort's gunpowder supply that the siege came to an end. In the tremendous explosion that followed, four fifths of the fort's inmates, women and children as well as men, died instantly. Only three escaped without some injury. The handful of survivors, who had been free farmers for two and three generations, were taken to Georgia and sold as slaves.

The maroons' peaceful days were at an end. Farmers from the Suwanee and other areas became outlaws and warriors. Joining with the Seminoles, they attacked U.S. forces wherever they could find them. General Jackson himself took the field with three thousand men and invaded Spanish Florida to wage what history books call the First Seminole War. It was full-scale warfare, with disciplined troops fighting on both sides. Negroes and Indians made a gallant, last-ditch stand on their farms along the Suwanee River but were defeated. General Jackson and his men burned their homes and cornfields and withdrew.

In 1819 the United States purchased Florida from Spain. Settlers from Georgia and South Carolina began to pour across the border and the maroons and Seminoles were forced to move. They gave up their bottom lands along the rivers and retreated to the hammocks and saw-grass swamps of the Everglades. There they built thatched huts, ate turtle and broiled fish, and gathered oranges and limes from trees that the Spanish had planted.

But even in the Everglades white planters considered them a threat. "The maroon Negroes fear being again made slaves," one observer explained, "and will omit nothing to increase or keep alive mistrust among the Indians, whom they, in fact, govern. It will be necessary to remove from the Floridas this group of freebooters, among whom runaway Negroes will always find a refuge."

General Jackson, then Florida's territorial governor, agreed. For more than twenty years, through a Second and a Third Seminole War, the United States Government fought to re-enslave the maroons and transport the Seminoles to lands west of the Mississippi.

Although the Negroes did not govern the Indians, who far outnumbered them, they were in the forefront of the struggle. Negro leaders visited the settlers' plantations at night—and slaves ran off by the hundreds to the Seminole camps. Negro warriors took the field, tomahawks in hand and war paint on their faces. Negro spies slipped back and forth through enemy lines with information and arms.

When Major Francis Dade was assigned to lead troops through the forest to Fort King, he hired a Tampa slave, Louis Pacheco, as his guide. Owned by a Florida widow, Louis was "good-looking and intelligent, able to read and write." He spoke English, French, Spanish, and Seminole. Intelligent Louis immediately sent word to the Indians that he planned to lead the soldiers past Great Wahoo Swamp.

By the time the troops reached Great Wahoo,

Indians and maroons were hiding behind every tree
along the trail. Dade and his company were wiped
out. Louis, who had thrown himself to the ground at
the first burst of fire, lay in the tall grass until the
battle was over and it was safe to identify himself.
That evening he translated the papers found on the
officers' bodies, giving the Indians valuable knowledge of United States plans.

During the next years Louis fought with the
Seminoles. When he was finally forced to emigrate to
the West, Mrs. Pacheco, his former owner, stepped
forward to claim him as her slave. The army thought
him too dangerous to return, however. "It would be
better to pay any price for such a man and leave
him in Arkansas, or hang him, than return him to the
borders of Florida," one officer testified.

Abraham was another well-known "Indian Negro"
who had run away to the Seminoles when he was a
boy. He became "sense-bearer" to Chief Micanopy
—a combination of secretary and chief counselor—and
married the widow of another chief. Over six feet
tall, with a slight mustache, he was called Yobly
by the Indians. "He always smiles and his words
flow like oil," a United States soldier said. "His conversation is soft and low but very distinct."

During the many treaty negotiations—treaties
which were signed and broken by both sides—Abraham was Micanopy's spokesman and interpreter. In
1826 he headed a Seminole delegation to Washington. Six years later he visited Arkansas to look over
the proposed Indian territory. Throughout the war

years he took the lead in urging resistance to the U.S. forces. But in 1837, when it was clear that the Seminoles could not hold out much longer, he made a dramatic appearance in the enemy camp, carrying a white flag on a stick and walking to the tent of General Jessup "with perfect dignity and composure."

"He is the Negro chief," Jessup said, "and the most cunning and intelligent Negro we have here. He claims to be free."

It was a claim which the general felt bound to respect. When an agreement was signed later in the year one section read: "Major General Jessup, in behalf of the United States, agrees that the Seminoles and their allies who come in and emigrate West shall be secure in their lives and property."

The costly Seminole Wars seemed to be over. Twenty-six ships gathered at Tampa Bay to transport the emigrants to New Orleans and beyond. Seven hundred maroons and Indians surrendered and more were trickling in every day.

Then the news that Jessup had agreed to ship the Negroes to Indian territory reached the planters. They stormed the general's camp, demanding that he return the maroons who were descendants of slaves who had run away from their fathers and grandfathers.

Jessup threw up his hands. "If the citizens of the territory be prudent the war may be considered at an end," he wrote to the governor of Florida. "But any attempt to interfere with the Indian Negroes would cause an immediate resort to arms. The arrival of two or three citizens of Florida, said to be in search of Negroes, caused them to disperse, and I doubt whether they will come in again; at all events the emigration will be delayed a month in consequence of this alarm among the Negroes."

But the citizens refused to be prudent. Soon Jessup was writing, "All is lost, and principally I fear by the influence of the Negroes." The war, which had taken the lives of thousands of men, was starting all over again.

Pushing farther and farther into Indian country, United States soldiers floundered in the black muck of the swamps and fell dead in the waving saw grass of the glades. Indian chiefs were captured and carried off to prison in Charleston. So many Negroes were held under guard at Tampa Bay that the town began to resemble an African slave factory. More than five hundred, most of them freeborn, were sold into slavery. Hundreds of others were transported to Cherokee lands in the West, to wander from there, always a day or two ahead of slave dealers, until they found freedom in Mexico.

The war continued. The last federal troops withdrew from Florida in 1843, but there were still bands of Seminoles and maroons hiding in the Everglades. Some of their descendants live there today, proud of the fact that they never surrendered to the Army of the United States.

A Declaration of Independence

Is life so dear, or peace so sweet, as to be purchased at the price of chains and slavery? Forbid it, Almighty God! I know not what course others may take, but as for me, give me liberty, or give me death!

—PATRICK HENRY

BY THE middle of the eighteenth century the slaves in British America were not alone in "calling out liberty." Their masters used the word too. At first it was liberty of the pocketbook that interested the colonists. They wanted freedom to trade with other countries besides England, freedom to manufacture their own goods instead of buying at high prices from London merchants. They wanted freedom from unfair taxes, from Sugar and Stamp acts and the hateful duty on tea.

Sons of Liberty burned stamps on the streets of New York and dumped chests of tea into Boston Harbor. Daughters of Liberty wore homespun gowns instead of "Gewgaws and exuberant Fineries" from

abroad, and brewed coffee over their kitchen fires.
In South Carolina colonists raided the homes of His
Majesty's agents and solemnly renounced the wearing of wigs. In conservative Philadelphia a lawyer
composed America's first patriotic song:

> In Freedom we're born and in Freedom we'll live.
> Our purses are ready.
> Steady, Friends, steady.
> Not as Slaves but as Free men our money we'll give.

For ten tumultuous years the colonists rioted, boycotted, argued, and sang. The fight against the King's
laws took shape as a fight against the King. Slowly
the talk in the coffeehouses turned from free trade to
free men.

"Every man is individually independent," James
Otis declared. "His right to his life, his liberty, and
his property no created being can rightfully contest."

"Among the natural rights of the colonists are
these," Samuel Adams explained. "First, a right to
life, secondly to liberty, thirdly to property."

"We are all born free," young Thomas Jefferson
wrote.

The slaves listened. Did the Boston patriots and
the Virginia gentleman mean that *all* men were born
free? Was a slave a man?

When the commander of the British forces in New
York declared that he would cram stamps down the
throats of the colonists with his sword, slaves joined
the Sons of Liberty in an attack on his garrison.
When British troops were sent to Boston to keep

KILDEER COUNTRYSIDE SCHOOL
R. 2
LONG GROVE, ILLINOIS

order, a runaway slave led the fight against the hated "lobsterbacks."

In an advertisement in a Boston newspaper, Crispus Attucks' master had described him as "6 Feet 2 Inches high, short curl'd Hair, his knees nearer together than common. Whoever shall take up said Run-away, shall have ten Pounds Reward, and all necessary Charges paid." But Attucks was never taken up. For twenty years he had shipped on Nantucket whalers, living the life of a free man. The winter of 1770 found him on shore leave in Boston.

Tension in the town was at a boiling point. Colonists and British soldiers were engaged in daily brawls. On the evening of March 5 a soldier struck a boy with the butt end of a musket and angry colonists retaliated by pelting the redcoats with snowballs.

Crispus Attucks mounted a box in Dock Square. "The way to get rid of these soldiers is to attack the main guard," he shouted.

"To the main guard!"

All along the street men echoed his cry. Someone climbed through the window of the Old Brick Meetinghouse and rang the bell. Crowds poured from nearby homes, following Attucks around the corner to the guard's headquarters on King Street. For an electric moment they faced each other—His Majesty's soldiers, trim in their scarlet uniforms, muskets primed, His Majesty's subjects with sticks and snowballs in their hands.

"Why do you hesitate?" Attucks rallied his followers. "They dare not fire."

Sticks struck against bayonets. "Fire and be damned," the crowd challenged.

"Fire!" The redcoats took up the challenge and the tall, knock-kneed sailor pitched forward onto the cobblestoned street. When the smoke cleared four Americans were dead.

British troops were hastily withdrawn from Boston, while Crispus Attucks lay in state in Faneuil Hall. "The Shops in Town were shut, all the Bells were ordered to toll a solemn Peal," and "an immense Concourse of People, so numerous as to be obliged to follow in Ranks of six," accompanied him to his grave.

The Boston Massacre helped to rally the colonists against their British rulers. "Not the Battle of Lexington or Bunker Hill, not the surrender of Burgoyne or Cornwallis were more important events in American history," John Adams said, "than the battle of King Street on the 5th of March, 1770."

All along the Atlantic seaboard patriot leaders began to stir uncomfortably in the presence of their brown-skinned bondsmen. When slaves in Charleston joined the struggle against the Stamp Act and echoed their masters' cries of "Liberty!" from British rule, South Carolinians were terrified. The militia was called out, strict curfews enforced, and slaves thrown into jail.

"I wish most sincerely there was not a slave in

the province," Abigail Adams wrote to her husband.
"It always appeared a most iniquitous scheme to me to
fight ourselves for what we are daily robbing and
plundering from those who have as good a right to
freedom as we have."

John Adams read her letter in Philadelphia as he
took his seat in the country's first Continental Congress. Slavery was not the burning issue of the day—
except to the slaves—but the slave trade had a place
on the long list of grievances against the English
crown. In Carpenters Hall in the fall of 1774 the
United Colonies decided to boycott British goods:
sugar, pimentos, wine, tea—and Negro slaves. In the
hope of injuring British business, they announced:

"We will neither import, nor purchase any Slave
imported after the First Day of December next; after
which Time, we will wholly discontinue the Slave
Trade, and will neither be concerned in it ourselves,
nor will we hire our Vessels, nor sell our Commodities or Manufactures to those who are concerned in
it."

The slaves listened, pulses quickening. This was
not an end to bondage, but it was a giant step in
that direction.

The United Colonies kept their agreement—for a
while. In South Carolina "a cargo of near three
hundred slaves was sent out of the Colony by the
consignee." In Virginia, Norfolk's Vigilance Committee held up "for your just indignation Mr. John
Brown, Merchant," who had imported slaves, "to the

end that all such foes to the rights of British America may be publickly known as the enemies of American Liberty."

The Battle of Lexington was fought and Paul Revere made his famous ride, but colonists still spoke of "British America." The majority of delegates to the Continental Congress thought of themselves as loyal subjects of His Majesty engaged in a temporary quarrel that would soon come to an end. Only a handful of radicals favored independence.

In a curious, backward sort of way, the issue of slavery helped to bring about the final break between the colonies and England. It began when Lord Dunmore, Virginia's royal governor, issued an emancipation proclamation!

"I do hereby declare," he announced in the fall of 1775, "all indented servants, Negroes or others (appertaining to the Rebels) free, that are able and willing to bear arms, they joining His Majesty's troops, as soon as may be, for the more speedily reducing this Colony to a proper sense of their duty to His Majesty's Crown and dignity."

As slaves flocked to him by the thousands, wild rumors spread through all the Southern colonies. Lord Dunmore was arming the slaves "for the glorious purpose of enticing them to cut their masters' throats," one newspaper reported. The King had promised that every Negro who murdered his owner would receive his plantation as a reward, angry planters said.

At the headquarters of the Continental Army, General Washington worried about Lord Dunmore's "diabolical scheme." "If that man is not crushed before spring, he will become the most formidable enemy America has," he wrote to his friend Richard Henry Lee.

By spring Southern conservatives and Northern radicals were close to agreement. In the State House in Philadelphia, Richard Henry Lee rose to his feet to offer a resolution in the name of Virginia's delegation:

"That these United Colonies are and of right ought to be, free and Independent States."

Before a vote was taken Congress gave Thomas Jefferson the job of putting down on paper their reasons for wanting independence. Jefferson's assignment, he later explained, was "not to find out new principles, or new arguments, but to place before mankind the common sense of the subject. It was intended to be an expression of the American mind."

The young lawyer from Virginia climbed the narrow stairs to his rooms on Market Street, pondering the problem. With his writing box open on his table, he set to work. First, a general statement concerning the rights of all men. Then a careful listing of the King's tyrannous acts.

Running his fingers through his red hair, Jefferson wrote slowly. Each word was weighed, each phrase polished, to give the statement "the proper tone and spirit called for by the occasion." When his final draft was finished he had listed more than two dozen charges against the King. The last of these said:

"He has waged cruel war against human nature itself, violating its most sacred rights of life and liberty in the persons of a distant people who never offended him, captivating and carrying them into slavery in another hemisphere. . . . This piratical warfare . . . is the warfare of the *Christian* king of Great Britain. Determined to keep open a market where MEN should be bought and sold . . . he is now exciting these very people to rise in arms against us. . . ."

Were slaves men? In this first "expression of the American mind," Jefferson, owner of almost two hundred slaves on his Virginia plantation, had decided that they were.

Congress thought otherwise. On the third and fourth of July 1776 delegates from the thirteen colonies met to discuss Jefferson's statement. They changed a phrase here and there, but there were no real objections until the secretary read the final charge against the King. Then tempers flared and the white-paneled walls of the State House echoed with angry arguments.

In the end the entire paragraph about slavery was cut out, "in complaisance to South Carolina and Georgia," Jefferson noted. "Our Northern brethren also I believe felt a little tender under these censures; for though their people have very few slaves themselves yet they had been pretty considerable carriers of them to others."

It was late on the afternoon of the fourth when the last changes were agreed on. The secretary called the roll and one by one the delegates rose to cast their vote. The Declaration of Independence was adopted unanimously.

Four days later the Declaration was read to the citizens of the new United States. A crowd jammed the yard behind the State House—shopkeepers, farmers, mechanics, sailors, Indians, and Negro slaves.

". . . We hold these Truths to be self-evident, that all men are created equal, that they are endowed by their Creator with certain inalienable rights, that among these are Life, Liberty and the Pursuit of Happiness. That to secure these rights, Governments are instituted among Men, deriving their just powers from the consent of the governed. That whenever any Form of Government becomes destructive of these ends, it is the Right of the People to alter or to abolish it, and to institute new Government. . . ."

Even without the section on slavery, these were stirring words. For the first time in the history of the world a nation was founded on the principles of freedom and equality. Cannon boomed, bells rang, and people paraded through the streets cheering and shouting. In the evening they set off fireworks and built bonfires to burn the King's flags and arms.

The slaves listened, hearts swelling with hope. In that summer of '76 they learned to whistle "Yankee Doodle."

Revolution!

In the cause of my black brethren I feel myself warmly interested. Whatever be the complexion of the enslaved, it does not, in my opinion, alter the complexion of the crime which the enslaver commits, a crime much blacker than any African face.

—MARQUIS DE LAFAYETTE

IT WAS one thing to declare independence, another to win it by force of arms from the strongest military and naval power in the world. For seven desperate years Americans fought for their freedom. All kinds of Americans fought.

There were Negro Minute Men at Lexington, Concord, and Bunker Hill. Negro Green Mountain Boys fought at Fort Ticonderoga with Ethan Allen. Negro soldiers crossed the icy Delaware River with George Washington and bled and died in the snow at Valley Forge.

Men with brown skins were not always welcomed in the American Army. When General Washington first took command he told recruiting officers not to enlist "any stroller, Negro, or vagabond." This order stood until Lord Dunmore issued his emancipation proclamation. Then, alarmed by the likelihood of Negroes joining forces with the British, Washington decided to enlist free Negroes "but no others." The ban on "others" lasted for only a short time. Connecticut was soon enrolling "slaves of good life and conversation" and Rhode Island, Massachusetts, and New York raised Negro battalions with the promise that slaves who passed muster would be "absolutely made free."

Negro soldiers fought in almost every battle of the war, from the Battle of Rhode Island where they three times turned back the Hessians, to the siege of Savannah where black men from Haiti tried to rescue the city. There were Negro sailors on American gunboats and even a woman who served for seventeen months with a Massachusetts regiment and was commended for her "extraordinary instance of female heroism."

Most dramatic of all were the exploits of Negro spies. In 1779 Washington sent General Anthony Wayne to capture the British garrison at Stony Point, New York. The British had built breastworks high above the Hudson River. They called their position "Little Gibraltar." It would be impossible to take Stony Point by storm, Wayne informed Washington. "But perhaps a surprise may be effected."

The surprise was arranged by Pompey, a slave from a nearby farm. He paid daily visits to the garrison, making friends with the soldiers and peddling strawberries and cherries to the officers' mess. When he had won their confidence he regretfully informed them that his master had forbidden daytime visits because it was the season for hoeing corn. Rather than lose his fruit and company, the British taught him their countersign and ordered the sentries to pass him at night.

One warm summer evening Pompey arrived as usual with his basket of fruit slung over his arm. While he chatted with a sentry two of Wayne's soldiers seized and gagged the red-coated guard. After a second sentinel was disposed of in the same way the Americans captured the garrison and its six hundred men. Congress gave a gold medal to General Wayne; Pompey received freedom and a horse.

Another slave, James Armistead, played the dangerous role of counterspy. When the Marquis de Lafayette faced Cornwallis in Virginia, Armistead volunteered to visit the British camp to learn their plans. While there, he so impressed Cornwallis that the British general enlisted him to spy on Lafayette. Shuttling back and forth between the two camps, he carried correct information to the Americans and false to the British.

One day he gave Cornwallis some torn pieces of paper which he said he had picked up in Lafayette's camp. Putting the scraps together, Cornwallis was surprised to read of an increase in American strength. Because of this paper he called off a planned attack —which was exactly what Lafayette had hoped he would do! When the Revolution was over the Virginia legislature gave Armistead "as full freedom as if he had been born free" and the ex-slave changed his name to James Lafayette.

Of all of the states, only South Carolina and Georgia refused to enlist Negro soldiers. With more than half of its population slave, South Carolina had trouble raising its share of troops. But when Colonel John Laurens, a slaveowner from Charleston, proposed to form Negro regiments, his plan was angrily rejected.

By 1779 the need for troops in the South was so pressing that Congress urged Georgia and South Carolina to enlist three thousand slaves who would be freed at the end of the war. They even offered to pay a thousand dollars to the owner of each slave soldier out of the slender federal treasury.

Rice and indigo planters who, for a century, had maintained armed patrols to guard their slaves were not going to put guns in black men's hands. Not even if American independence was at stake. Some planters were so disturbed by Congress' resolution that they sent a flag of truce to the nearest British garrison and proposed that South Carolina remain neutral for the rest of the war.

Nevertheless, Laurens continued to battle for his "black project." "I was outvoted," he wrote two years later, "having only reason on my side and being opposed by avarice, prejudice, and pusillanimity."

"I must confess that I am not at all astonished at

the failure of your plan," General Washington commented. "That spirit of freedom which at the commencement of this contest would have gladly sacrificed everything, has long since subsided, and every selfish passion has taken its place."

The British were quick to take advantage of South Carolina's weakness. Charleston fell in 1780, with scarcely a shot fired in its defense, and the royal colors flew over the city until the war ended. Georgia shared the same fate, despite a gallant attempt on the part of French and Northern troops to liberate Savannah.

Forbidden to shoulder arms, the slaves ran away. Georgians complained that three fourths of their slave property disappeared during the Revolution. South Carolinians estimated their losses at more than twenty-five thousand. Many of these slaves hid in maroon camps in the back country or made their way to Florida. Others fought on the side of the British. As late as 1786 bands of former slaves, calling themselves the King of England's Soldiers, were raiding plantations along the Savannah River.

By the time the Treaty of Paris recognized the United States as an independent nation, its slave system was thoroughly shaken. Five thousand Negroes had fought in the army and navy. Thousands of others had served as spies, wagoners, workers on fortifications.

One fifth of all the slaves in the country had run away from their masters. Thirty of Thomas Jefferson's slaves joined Cornwallis when he invaded Virginia. Several of George Washington's men fled to British ships in New York Harbor. Richard Henry Lee wrote that two neighhors had "lost every slave they had in the world. This has been the general case of all those who were near the enemy." Even in upstate New York, far from the front lines, there were mass flights of slaves to Canada.

The idea of liberty and equality for all was beginning to conquer "that monstrous popular prejudice" against men with dark skins. All Negroes were no longer salt-water Africans like Kamba. Some of their ancestors had lived in America for one hundred and fifty years. In spite of cruel oppression and limited opportunity for education, more and more of them were commanding the respect of the citizens of the new Republic.

Benjamin Banneker was an American. The grandson of an African chief who had gained his freedom, Banneker astonished his Maryland neighbors by building the first clock in the colony. Later he built an observatory with a window in his cabin roof so that he could study the stars even on the coldest nights. When a Quaker friend loaned him books on mathematics and astronomy he mastered them so thoroughly that he was able to predict both local weather and eclipses of the sun.

As the news of his mathematical ability spread, he was asked to be a member of the team of surveyors who laid out the new federal city of Washington. When he was in his sixties he edited a series of popular almanacs which contained weather forecasts, tide tables, essays, and verse.

"To make an Almanac is not so easy a matter as some people think," his publisher announced. "To whom do you think you are indebted for this entertainment? Why to a Black Man—Strange! Is a Black capable of compiling an Almanac? Indeed it is no less strange than true; and a clever, wise longheaded Black he is."

Banneker sent his first almanac to Thomas Jefferson, boldly pointing out that his achievement contradicted the notion that Negroes were "brutish" rather than human. Jefferson forwarded it to the Academy of Sciences in Paris so that scientists could see proof "that nature has given to our black brethren talents equal to those of other colours of men."

Phillis Wheatley was an American. Born in Africa, she was sold on the streets of Boston when she was eight years old. Her master and mistress were kind and she was treated almost as a member of their family. Taught by their daughter, she surprised the New England colonists by learning Latin and writing poetry. Her first book of poems was published in London when she was twenty. At the beginning of the Revolution she addressed a poem to "His Excellency General Washington":

. . . Proceed, great chief, with virtue on thy side,
Thy ev'ry action let the goddess guide.
A crown, a mansion, and a throne that shine,
With gold unfading, *Washington!* be thine.

Praising her "poetical talents," the general invited "Miss Phillis" to pay him a visit. In the winter of '76 the slave girl and the Commander-in-Chief met for a half hour's talk at Continental Army headquarters in Cambridge.

Paul Cuffe was an American. The son of an African father and an Indian mother, he spent his boyhood on New Bedford whaling ships. From a small open boat which he built himself, he became the owner of a fleet of sailing vessels that crisscrossed the ocean. During the Revolution he joined other free Negroes in a protest against taxation without representation. They refused to pay taxes because "We are not allowed the Privilage of freemen of the State having no vote or Influence in the Election of those that Tax us." Recognizing the justice of the complaint, the Massachusetts General Court gave Negro taxpayers the same rights as their white fellow citizens.

John Chavis was an American. When he was a boy in North Carolina, two white men had an argument. One claimed that Negroes could not be educated. The other was equally sure that they could. To settle their wager, Chavis was sent to Princeton, then the College of New Jersey. After he returned home trained as a minister and teacher, his backer gleefully collected his bet.

For almost thirty years John Chavis headed the best-known school in North Carolina. His pupils included future judges, lawyers, doctors, and one state governor. During the daytime hours he taught white children. At night he gave lessons to the sons and daughters of freed slaves.

By the end of the Revolution, many Americans believed that Negroes were entitled to their freedom. Pennsylvania Quakers had formed a Society for Promoting the Abolition of Slavery with Benjamin Franklin as its president and Thomas Paine and Lafayette among its prominent members. Chief Justice John Jay headed a similar society in New York and anti-slavery groups were organizing in almost every state.

When the first United States census was taken in 1790, Massachusetts was able to write a proud "NONE" in the column headed "Number of Slaves." All of her Northern neighbors were passing laws for the gradual emancipation of their human property. Some of these laws were very gradual indeed. New York had slaves until 1827, New Jersey as late as 1846. But slavery as an institution was clearly on its last legs in the North.

In the Middle States, too, it seemed to be tottering. One after another, Delaware, Virginia, Maryland, North Carolina prohibited the importation of slaves from Africa and considered bills for emancipation. The Black Codes—laws governing the conduct of slaves—became more lenient, and masters who wished to give their slaves freedom were permitted to do so.

In 1785 Jefferson hoped that Virginia would be "the next state to which we may turn our eyes for the interesting spectacle of justice in conflict with avarice and oppression." He looked toward the young men who had "sucked in the principles of liberty as it were with their mother's milk to turn the fate of the question."

In those first heady years of independence the Revolutionary dream of freedom for all men seemed about to come true. Then the dream collided with harsh reality.

To Form a More Perfect Union

*The states were divided into different interests,
not by their difference of size, but by other considerations the most material of which resulted
partly from climate, but principally from the ef-
fects of their having or not having slaves.*

—JAMES MADISON

IN 1787 the nation's leaders traveled to Philadelphia to draw up a constitution for their new country.
Their business now was not revolution but the organization of a strong central government. None of
the radicals of the first Continental Congress were
present. The delegates to the Constitutional Convention were hardheaded men of affairs—lawyers, planters, merchants, bankers.

Meeting in the same room in which the Declaration
of Independence had been signed, they elected
George Washington as their presiding officer. Sessions
were held in secret, with armed sentries posted at the
door. Delegates pledged themselves not to give out
information on the proceedings and tried to keep an

eye on talkative Benjamin Franklin to make sure that
he told no state secrets at his evening dinner parties.
To complete the hush-hush atmosphere, the pave-
ment in front of the State House was spread with
loose earth, so that squeaking cartwheels and horses'
hoofbeats would not disturb the deliberations.

For three sweltering summer months the delegates
tackled the problem of welding thirteen separate colonies into a truly United States. There were thorny
questions to be settled. Should Congress have two
houses or one? Should large states be given more
power than small? How should a President be chosen?
Should the states or the nation regulate taxes, tariffs,
trade? Even a motion to open the daily sessions with
prayer was vigorously debated and finally voted down.

Whether it was right or wrong to own slaves was
never a part of the Convention's business. No dele-
gate proposed that slavery be abolished, even at some
distant future date. Yet slavery was present at each
Convention session like a ghost at the feast.

Take taxes, for instance. Early in the war Congress
had decided to tax each state according to the number of its inhabitants. Should slaves be counted as
inhabitants?

"No," said the representative from South Carolina.
"Our slaves are property. They are no more to be
taxed than sheep."

Peering over the top of his spectacles, Benjamin
Franklin begged to disagree. "There is some differ-
ence between them and sheep," he slyly pointed out.
"Sheep will never make any insurrections."

Slaves had not been counted for the purpose of wartime taxation, but the issue arose again now. How many congressmen was each state entitled to? Delegates readily agreed that the number of representatives must depend on a state's population. Should slaves be counted as people?

This time South Carolina and Georgia said, "Yes." If their slaves were counted they would have more representatives in Congress and a louder voice in the federal government.

There was an uproar from the North. "Upon what principle is it that the slaves shall be computed in the representation?" Gouverneur Morris of Pennsylvania demanded to know. "Are they men? Then make them citizens and let them vote. Are they property? Why, then, is no other property included? The houses in this city are worth more than all the wretched slaves that cover the rice swamps of South Carolina."

Delegates from Massachusetts and New Jersey backed him up. "In a meeting the slaves would not be allowed to vote. Why then should they be represented?"

But the South stood firm until a fateful compromise put an end to the argument. A census would be taken to learn the population of each state, in order to determine both taxes and representation in Congress. In this census, every slave would be counted —as three fifths of a man!

Next came a bitter wrangle over the question of the importation of slaves from Africa. In 1774 the United Colonies had agreed to end the slave trade. In

1776 the Continental Congress resolved that "no slave be imported into any of the United States." Now delegates from South Carolina and Georgia flatly stated that they would "not be parties to the Union unless their right to import slaves be untouched."

"Religion and humanity have nothing to do with this question," John Rutledge of South Carolina said. "If the Northern states consult their interest they will not oppose the increase of slaves, which will increase the commodities of which they will become the carriers."

"South Carolina and Georgia cannot do without slaves," his colleagues added. "If the Convention thought" that they would agree to end importations "the expectation is vain."

One by one, delegates from the Middle and Northern states rose to denounce the slave trade. "Infernal," said Mason of Virginia. "Dishonorable," said Martin of Maryland. "Nefarious," said Morris of Pennsylvania. "Iniquitous," said Sherman of Connecticut.

Then, one by one, they sat down to listen thoughtfully to what the South had to say.

We are opposed to government "meddling with the importation of Negroes," Charles Pinckney explained. But, he added, "if the states be all left at liberty on this subject, South Carolina may perhaps by degrees do of herself what is wished."

This sounded hopeful. "Let us not intermeddle," Ellsworth of Connecticut prudently advised. "The

morality or wisdom of slavery are considerations belonging to the states."

All over the chamber, heads nodded. "It's better to
let the Southern states import slaves than to part with
them," Roger Sherman pointed out.

Soon a committee was organized to work out another compromise. It didn't take long to strike a bargain. A portion of the navigation acts that New England merchants disliked was cut out. In return, the
Constitution forbade Congress to "meddle" with the
slave trade for twenty years. The question could not
even be discussed again until 1807.

Three days later, when a section requiring the return of runaway slaves to their owners was proposed,
there were scarcely any objections from Northern delegates. Only one small nicety remained to be settled.

The preamble to the Constitution spoke of estab-
lishing justice and securing "the blessings of liberty."
It was jarring to speak of justice, liberty, and slavery
in the same breath. Expressing the embarrassment
that many of his fellow delegates felt, James Madison of Virginia "thought it wrong to admit in the
Constitution the idea of property in men."

Nothing could be simpler to arrange. "Slavery" and
"slave" were carefully erased from the document and
vague phrases put in their place. The Constitution
spoke of counting "three-fifths of *all other persons*,"
of importing "*Such persons* as any of the States . . .
shall think proper to admit." A runaway slave was
called a "*person held to Service or Labour.*" His

master was "*the Party* to whom such Service or Labour may be due." The words were changed, but everyone understood their meaning.

The first leaves were falling from the mulberry tree
in Benjamin Franklin's back yard when the delegates
signed their names to the parchment scroll and set
out for home. In succeeding months a majority of
states approved the Constitution and in the spring of
1789 George Washington traveled to New York to
take office as the first President of the United States.

Until the Constitution was drawn up, slavery
could be blamed on English merchants and the English King. Now it was recognized in the law of the
land. It was established as a thoroughly American institution.

Almost to a man, the founding fathers of the new
Republic opposed slavery. Only months before the
Convention Washington had wished "to see some
plan adopted by which slavery may be abolished by
slow, sure and imperceptible degrees."

"This abomination must have an end," Jefferson was
writing at the same time. "There is a superior bench
reserved in heaven for those who hasten it."

Yet almost to a man, the founding fathers were
slaveowners. Of the first seven Presidents, only the Ad-
amses could say, "I have never owned a Negro."

Jefferson's "people," living in brick homes on his
Monticello estate, were perhaps the best-cared-for
slaves in the country. But even the author of the Dec-

laration of Independence did not hesitate to sell them when he needed money to pay pressing debts.

Close to three hundred slaves worked on Washington's farm at Mount Vernon. He was a strict taskmaster who advertised for runaways and sold rebellious field hands to planters in the West Indies. In his last years he resolved not to buy or sell slaves, "unless some particular circumstance should compel me to it . . . because I am principled against this kind of traffic in the human species." In his will he provided for his slaves' gradual emancipation and education "to some useful occupation."

Patrick Henry also expressed an uneasy conscience about slavery. "Every thinking man rejects it in Speculation, how few in practice?" he asked. "Would anyone believe that I am Master of slaves of my own purchase? I am drawn along by ye general Inconvenience of Living without them. I will not, I cannot justify it."

In the first years of the Republic, scarcely anyone attempted to justify slavery. But the need for a united prosperous country, as well as the "general inconvenience" of living without slave labor, came before questions of conscience. These could be taken up again in 1807. Then, when the African slave trade was ended, surely slavery would disappear.

Emancipation of the slaves had not been forgotten by the men who signed the Declaration of Independence. It had merely been postponed for twenty years.

Twenty years turned out to be too long.

A Positive Good

FOR SALE, a wench and four
  female children.
CASH will be given for 12 or
  15 boys, from 7 to 15 years
  old.
I wish to purchase 50 Negroes
  of both sexes from 6 to 30
  years of age.
A good bargain may be had for
  cash. She is in her 7th
  year, well grown, healthy
  and strong.

—Advertisements in
Southern Newspapers

On New Year's Day in 1809, Negroes in the North held a Jubilee of Liberty. In New York City a grand marshal on a milk-white horse led a parade down Broadway. Horns tooted, bands played, banners waved. Thousands of men and women, dressed in their Sunday best, marched through the streets to Liberty Hall. At the end of the procession two men carried a life-size portrait of a slave with a legend asking Am I not a man and a brother?

The paraders were celebrating the end of the African slave trade. A year earlier Congress had passed a

law forbidding the importation of slaves into any
United States port. When the British Parliament
passed a similar law, anti-slavery men everywhere met
for speeches and song.

But it was too late for a Jubilee of Liberty—or too
soon. Many things had changed in the years since
the Constitutional Convention. The purchase of the
Louisiana Territory had doubled the area of the
United States. The new country was beginning to
play an important part in world affairs. Its ambassadors were in every European court. Its industries
were growing and its merchant vessels sailing the
seven seas.

Perhaps the greatest change of all had taken place
in the South, where a Yankee schoolteacher's inven-
tion of the cotton gin altered the face of the land.
Until Eli Whitney spent a winter on a Georgia plantation, Southerners depended on tobacco and rice for
a poor livelihood. Only a handful of men raised cotton because it was too expensive to separate the seeds
from the fluffy white fibers. After Whitney's cotton
gin took over this time-consuming work a new road
to riches was suddenly opened.

Cotton was easy to grow in the warm climate of the
South. It needed only land and laborers. Each year
planters bought more cotton acres. From the coast,
they spilled over into the back country of the Carolinas, across the piny woods of Georgia and Alabama
to the rich black soil of the Louisiana Territory. Each
year they bought more slaves. Black hands plowed

the soil and planted the seeds, weeded, picked, ginned, and baled the precious fibers.

Cotton was easy to grow and easy to sell. In England and New England, factories were springing up on every riverbank. As water power and steam were harnessed to machines, cotton could be transformed into cloth for people all over the world. In 1776 the South raised a million pounds of cotton. In 1809 the figure was eighty-six million, and this was only the beginning. Cotton prices soared—and so did the price of slaves.

While planters dreamed of a never ending pyramid of cotton bales, it is not surprising that the law ending the African slave trade was a halfhearted law, enforced halfheartedly. Tens of thousands of Africans were smuggled into the country through Florida and Gulf Coast ports. In Southern cities they were openly advertised for sale as "Negroes who never learned to talk English." Sometimes pirates flying black flags landed their booty on islands near the Southern coast. More often, respectable shipmasters from New England and wealthy New York merchants conspired with planters to evade the law.

Most of the recruits in the growing slave army did not come from Africa, however. While planters in the Deep South raised cotton, planters in the Middle States raised slaves. In Virginia and Maryland a crop of dark-skinned children was more profitable than tobacco or corn. Expenses were low—only eight or nine dollars a year for food and clothing—and prices high.

A Virginia planter, pleased because his slave girls were "uncommonly good breeders," said that each one of their babies "was worth two hundred dollars the moment it drew breath."

Slaves had been sold from plantation to plantation before when masters needed money, but this was new. This was an organized business of breeding, buying, shipping, selling, which wiped out Negro family life. It was an everyday occurrence for husbands to be sold away from wives, and children away from parents.

A practical preacher in Kentucky married slave couples, "until death or *distance* do you part." A slave from Mississippi said, "Most folks can't remember many things happened to 'em when they only eight years old, but that was when I was took away from my own mammy and pappy and sent off and bound out to another man, 'way off two-three hundred miles away. And that's the last time I ever see either one of them, or any my own kinfolks!"

Throughout the Middle States planters offered prizes to slave mothers who had the most children. Buyers with CASH FOR NEGROES signs on their hats toured the countryside looking for bargains. There was scarcely a town without its slave market and jail, "well supplied with thumbscrews and gags and ornamented with cowskins and other whips," a newspaper editor wrote.

As soon as the buyers assembled a likely-looking collection of slaves they headed South. The largest trading firms owned fleets of ships, sailing fortnightly from Baltimore or Norfolk with men bolted to the decks or stowed two deep in the hold. Others sent their merchandise overland, on foot.

Long lines of slaves shuffled along the highways, women and children fastened to rope halters, men handcuffed to long chains. When they passed through towns the trader ordered them to "step lively" or sent a slave fiddler to the head of the line to lead in a song. Some were sold along the way, but for most the long march ended on the auction block in Memphis or New Orleans.

The auctioneer mounted the platform, cracking jokes as he praised his produce. "Did you all ever see a finer lot'n this here boy? He's only twelve years old. In four years he'll be bigger'n me. He kin hoe cotton or corn, drive, wait, run errands, learn any trade. . . . Will you make it five-fifty? . . . Say six, make it six hundred. . . . Here, boy, show them gentlemen how you kin run. . . . Seven hundred? . . . Once-twice-third and last call. Going, going . . ." His right hand struck the palm of his left and the boy was "sold to Mr. Jenks for $700."

The twelve-year-old Virginian sold to Mr. Jenks of Mississippi was scarcely any better off than Kamba had been a century earlier. True, he could speak English, but he was separated forever from family and home and sentenced to a lifetime of hard labor.

"The conch shell blowed afore daylight," a slave recalled, "and all hands better git out for roll call, or Solomon bust the door down and git them out. It was work hard, git beatings, and half-fed. They brung the victuals and water to the fields on a slide pulled by a old mule. Plenty times they was only a half barrel water and it stale and hot, for all us Negroes on the hottest days. Mostly we ate pickled pork and corn bread and peas and beans and 'taters. They never was as much as we needed."

Boys and girls were considered particularly good buys at the slave auctions because they were easier to break in. Usually they were sent to the fields when they were five or six.

"Had to go round sticking slabs and branches in the fences where the hogs done pushed their heads through, till I was 'bout six years old. After that they put me in the field 'cause I was big an' strong for my age. Used to plow 'fore I could reach up to the handles. Would stick my head under the cross bar an' wrap my arms roun' the sides whilst another boy led the mule."

By ten, children were hoeing and picking cotton. At twelve, they were veteran workers, doing a man-sized job from dawn until after dark. Mississippi laws permitted an eighteen-hour workday for slaves, Georgia and Alabama nineteen. Mr. Jenks did not have to worry about supporting his slaves when they were too old to work, for statistics showed that the average Mississippi slave had a life expectancy of seventeen and a half years!

During the Constitutional Convention, only South

Carolina and Georgia had fought for the right to own slaves. As the slave army came to represent billions of dollars' worth of property, leaders in every Southern state stopped apologizing for slavery and began to justify it.

College professors "proved" that "The Negro is not equal to the white man." Ministers called slavery "the Lord's doing and marvelous in our eyes." Politicians dismissed the Declaration of Independence as a collection of "glittering generalities."

"I repudiate as ridiculously absurd that much lauded but nowhere accredited motto of Mr. Jefferson that 'all men are born free and equal,'" Governor Hammond of South Carolina declared.

"Slavery is a positive good," John Calhoun told the U. S. Senate. "Many once believed that it was a moral and political evil, but that folly and delusion are gone."

The Thunder Rolled

*From a small spark kindled in America a flame
has arisen, not to be extinguished.*
— THOMAS PAINE

WHILE the South tried to forget the Declaration
of Independence, sparks from this revolutionary document spread to other parts of the world. George
Washington had been President for only a few
months when revolution broke out in France. In the
French colony of San Domingo, slaves who listened
to their masters talk of "liberty, equality, and frater-
nity" declared themselves free. Led by Toussaint
L'Ouverture, a slave coachman, they fought for a
dozen bloody years until they had abolished slavery
and established the free Black Republic of Haiti.

The revolution in Haiti was only a thousand miles
from the South Carolina coast. Boatloads of Haitian
planters sought refuge in Charleston and Richmond.

Black men were slaughtering whites. Black men were defeating European-trained armies and forming a government of their own. If it could happen in Haiti, why not in the United States?

Frightened slaveowners tried frantically to keep the spark from spreading to their shores. Although the slave trade was still legal at that time, the Carolinas and Georgia promptly closed their ports to slave ships, and Congress passed a law banning trade with Haiti. Even when the Southern states began importing slaves again they refused to buy Negroes from the West Indian islands for fear that they might purchase a black revolutionary.

It was easier, however, to quarantine men than ideas. The slave who went to town for mail in the morning, the slave who drove his master's carriage, waited on table, or dusted the parlor of the Big House knew what was going on in the world. He no longer had the talking drums of Africa to carry the news, but he was part of a speedy and efficient grapevine. A Virginia slave explained the workings of the grapevine on her plantation:

"Was serving girl for Missus. Used to have to stand behind her at the table an reach her the salt an syrup an anything else she called for. Ole Marsa would spell out real fast anything he don't want me to know 'bout. One day was raving 'bout the crops, an taxes an the trifling Negroes he got to feed. 'Gonna sell 'em, I swear before Christ,' he says. Then ole Missus asks which ones he gonna sell and tell him quick to spell it. Then he spell out G-A-B-E and R-U-F-U-S.

"Course I stood there without batting an eye, an making believe I didn't even hear him, but I was packing them letters up in my head all the time. An soon's I finished dishes I rushed down to my father and says 'em to him just like Marsa say 'em. Father says quiet-like, 'Gabe and Rufus' an tole me to go on back to the house. The next day Gabe and Rufus was gone. They had run away. Marsa nearly died, got to cussing and raving so he took sick, but they never could find those two slaves."

Masters could spell from morning until night, but the name of Toussaint and the story of the Haitian revolution was known in every slave cabin from New Jersey to New Orleans.

Gabriel Prosser heard it while he was driving his master along the country roads of Virginia. Like Toussaint, Gabriel was a coachman, a giant of a man, with boundless courage and energy. Stirred by the reports from overseas, he conceived a daring plan for the deliverance of Virginia slaves.

Every Sunday for months he used his free hours to travel to Richmond. He mapped the roads that led to the state capital and noted the location of the arsenal and powder house. Slave blacksmiths began to turn scythe blades into swords. Slave carpenters made clubs from fence posts and Gabriel ordered a silk flag bearing the legend DEATH OR LIBERTY.

On the night of August 30, 1800, more than a thousand slaves, many of them on horseback, met at a brook six miles from Richmond. With General Gabriel at their head, three columns planned to march on the city. After capturing the arsenal, they would fan out until all of Richmond was theirs. In a day they expected to call on "their fellow Negroes and the friends of humanity throughout the continent" to join them. "If the white people agreed to their freedom they would then hoist a white flag."

With fifty thousand slaves in neighboring counties, they had every right to hope for success. But they failed.

"Upon that very evening, just about Sunset," an eyewitness said, "there came on the most terrible thunder, accompanied with an enormous rain, that I ever witnessed in this State." Hurricane winds blew down houses, rivers overflowed, bridges washed away. Gabriel's army, floundering in knee-deep mud, decided to postpone their attack for a day. By then it was too late. Two timid slaves confessed the plan to their master and James Monroe, Virginia's governor, called in federal troops.

The next weeks saw a desperate slave hunt throughout the state. Gabriel, described in newspaper advertisements as a "fellow of courage and intellect above his rank in life," escaped by boat to Norfolk. After a month of freedom he was recognized and taken back to Richmond to be hanged. Thirty-five slaves were executed, but other suspects were pardoned, "owing to the immense numbers who are interested in the plot, whose death will nearly produce the annihilation of the blacks in this part of the country."

One prisoner who was asked if he had anything to say in his defense replied with pride, "I have nothing more to offer than what General Washington would have had to offer, had he been taken by the British officers. I have ventured my life in endeavoring to obtain the liberty of my countrymen, and am a willing sacrifice to their cause; and I beg, as a favor, that I may be immediately led to execution."

In the same year that Gabriel organized his rebellion a South Carolina slave held the winning ticket in a lottery. With his $1500 prize money he bought his freedom. African-born Denmark Vesey was thirty-four years old when he went to work as a carpenter in the port city of Charleston. Energetic and thrifty, he prospered and became a man of substance in the community.

In his spare hours Vesey began to read and think and talk. Sometime around the year 1820 he decided to "see what he could do for his fellow-creatures." Getting in touch with groups of slaves in Charleston and on nearby plantations, he held secret meetings in his home. He told the slaves the story of Toussaint and "read from the Bible, how the Children of Israel were delivered out of Egypt from bondage." "If a colored man bowed to a white person," one of Vesey's comrades recalled, "he would rebuke him and observe that all men were born equal, and that he was surprised that anyone would degrade himself by such conduct."

It wasn't long before Vesey and his followers were making plans for a revolt. Thousands of slaves armed with homemade pikes and bayonets organized themselves into military companies. Coachmen and draymen promised to supply their masters' horses and a slave barber made wigs to disguise the leaders of the rebellion. With the help of a Negro sailor, Vesey smuggled out two letters to Haiti, asking the President of the black republic for assistance.

The uprising was scheduled for a Sunday in June in 1822. Weeks before, as word was passed along to subleaders, one of Vesey's lieutenants warned, "Take care and don't mention it to those men who receive presents of old coats from their masters, or they'll betray us." Despite this caution, a "favorite and confidential slave" learned of the plans and informed his master. One hundred and thirty-one Negroes and four white men were arrested. When red-hot wires were driven under their fingernails, a handful of the conspirators confessed. Most followed the advice of their leaders, who said, "Do not open your lips. Die silent."

With troops patrolling the streets of Charleston, the rebels were "strung up with as little ceremony as they string up fish in the Fulton Market," a New York newspaper wrote. Denmark Vesey's last words were a shout to the slaves to continue their struggle until they had won.

Slave unrest continued. The spark of freedom was hard to stamp out. Succeeding years saw revolts in

Georgia, Alabama, Louisiana, Maryland, Kentucky—and the most frightening of them all in Virginia.

Even as a child there was something about Nat Turner that made people believe that he "was intended for some great purpose." His mother, who had tried to kill him at birth rather than see him grow up in bondage, thought he "had too much sense to be raised and would never be of any service to anyone as a slave."

Nat was a prodigy who taught himself to read and whose unusual memory astonished black and white alike. "Whenever an opportunity occurred of looking at a book, when the schoolchildren were getting their lessons," he recalled, "I would find many things that the fertility of my own imagination had depicted to me before. All my time, not devoted to my master's service, was spent in making experiments in casting different things in moulds made of earth, in attempting to make paper, gunpowder, and many other experiments."

As he grew older, his interests turned from science to religion. A careful reading of the Bible convinced him that he was destined to lead the slaves to freedom. In a dream he saw "white spirits and black spirits engaged in battle, and the sun was darkened—the thunder rolled in the heavens and blood flowed in streams—and I heard a voice saying, 'Such is your luck, such you are called to see; and let it come rough or smooth, you must surely bear it.'"

Preaching to the slaves, baptizing them in the river

"when the white people would not let us be baptized by the church," he fasted and prayed for guidance. Like Joan of Arc, Nat Turner began to hear voices. Hers had counseled her to buckle on a sword and lead the army of France to victory. His told him that "Christ had laid down the yoke he had borne for the sins of men and that I should take it on. I should arise and prepare myself, and slay my enemies with their own weapons."

On a summer night in 1831, Nat Turner met with five disciples to plan a march on the nearby town of Jerusalem. Traveling from plantation to plantation, they killed slaveowners and collected axes, guns, and new recruits. By sunset on the following day more than seventy Negroes were on the march and sixty whites were dead.

There could be only one ending to Nat Turner's terrible crusade. Before he reached Jerusalem militiamen and cavalry from all over the state galloped to the planters' rescue. With the odds against them overwhelming, the slaves scattered to the woods.

When the massacre of the whites was over, the massacre of Negroes began. Scores of men who had nothing to do with the uprising were tortured and burned, their heads impaled on fences as a grisly warning. Fifty-five Negroes were brought to trial, but Nat Turner was still at large and no slaveowner in the South could rest. Every footstep breaking the silence of the night, every branch whipping against a curtained window seemed to threaten destruction.

While a thousand armed men combed the countryside looking for Nat, he hid only a few miles from home in a hole that he had dug out with his sword. For two months he remained in his homemade cave, coming out at night to forage for food. Betrayed by a barking dog who sniffed meat he had hidden, Nat managed to escape capture for still another fortnight. With a posse at his heels, he concealed himself in haystacks and under fallen trees. Weary and starved, he was forced at last to surrender his rusty sword. Seventy days after his crusade for freedom had begun he reached Jerusalem—in chains.

Even his capture brought panic to neighboring communities. When horsemen rode through the streets shouting, "Nat is caught," frightened white people ran for the swamps. They thought that they had heard "Nat is coming."

Crowds traveled from every county in Virginia to watch Nat Turner swing from the limb of a tree in Jerusalem's square. After the hanging his body was turned over to a surgeon for dissection. His flesh was boiled down for grease and bits of his skin and bones given away as souvenirs to members of the posse. Nat Turner was dead, his body systematically destroyed. But his spirit remained to haunt the South for thirty more years.

To the slaves, he became a legend, a Black Prophet who had risen once and might return. In the quarters they told stories about "ole Nat" or softly sang:

"You mought be rich as cream
And drive you a coach and four-horse team.
But you can't keep the world from moverin' around
And Nat Turner back from the gaining ground.

And your name it mought be Caesar sure,
And got you cannon can shoot a mile or more,
But you can't keep the world from moverin' around
And Nat Turner back from the gaining ground."

In the Big Houses slaveowners' voices trembled as
they talked of Gabriel and Vesey and the preacher
who had headed an avenging army. Now there was
"a suspicion that a Nat Turner might be in every family, that the same bloody deed might be acted over
at any time, that the materials for it were spread
through the land and were always ready for a like explosion."

Each rebellion was followed by a wave of fear that
was close by hysteria. In Virginia, "some have died,
others have become deranged from apprehension."
In North Carolina, the townspeople of Windsor heard
that nearby Winton had been burned to the ground.
Winton believed the same rumor about Windsor until messengers from the two communities met mid-
way on the highway and compared notes.

Alabamians built pens in the woods where they
planned to hide in case of slave rebellion. South Carolinians packed precious possessions in bags, "ready
to tote, if we heard they were coming our way." In
one village gunfire "alarmed the people very much.
They at once thought that the slaves had risen to

murder the white people. Many immediately left their houses and fled to the woods. It was afterwards ascertained that it was a false alarm." "It is a disagreeable state of living to be ever suspicious of those with whom we live," a Tennesseean complained.

It was indeed disagreeable—for all concerned. In Macon, Georgia, when citizens were awakened by rumors of a midnight attack, slaves were tied to trees and hacked to death. Suspected rebels were tortured in Mississippi, whipped in Texas, and hanged in Louisiana. In South Carolina the attorney general cautioned against too many executions. "I am afraid you will hang half the country," he said. "You must take care and save Negroes enough for the rice crop."

What could be done to restore peace to the embattled Southern countryside? "If we will keep a ferocious monster in our country, we must keep him in chains," a Virginia slaveholder said.

The Black Codes, which had been liberalized after the American Revolution, were tightened again. Armed men patrolled the roads at night, breaking into slave cabins to search for weapons. Slaves were forbidden to leave plantations without a written pass from their masters, or to hold meetings unless a white man was present. They could not own guns, beat drums, blow horns.

Denmark Vesey had been free. Therefore slaves could not visit free Negroes or entertain them in their quarters. Denmark Vesey had talked with Negro sailors from abroad. Therefore Negro crewmen must be jailed while their ships remained in South Carolina's ports.

Denmark Vesey and Nat Turner had used the Bible as a handbook for rebellion. Therefore Negro preachers and Negro churches were outlawed. Nat Turner was educated. Therefore no slaves could be taught to read and write. The punishment for studying was twenty lashes on the bare back. Even John Chavis, whose school had been in existence for a quarter of a century, was forced to abandon his night classes for Negroes.

Would these harsh measures work? When the Virginia Assembly met a month after Nat Turner's execution, one lawmaker expressed doubts. "Pass as severe laws as you will to keep these unfortunate creatures in ignorance, it is in vain unless you can extinguish that spark of intellect which God has given them," he warned. "I am not certain we would not do it if we could find out the necessary process. But this is impossible. Can man be in the midst of freedom and not know what freedom is?"

Oppressed So Hard

We raise the wheat, they give us the corn;
We bake the bread, they give us the crust;
We sift the meal, they give us the husk;
We peel the meat, they give us the skin;
And that's the way they take us in.
　　　　　　　　　　　—SLAVE SONG

As THE South became an armed camp, there was little hope for successful rebellion. Weaponless and outnumbered, slaves looked for new paths to freedom.

In the cities, blacksmiths and barbers, cooks and carpenters were sometimes permitted to "hire their own time." As Frederick Douglass explained it: "I was to be allowed to find my own employment, and to collect my own wages. In return for this liberty, I was required to pay three dollars at the end of each week, and to board and clothe myself, and buy my own tools. Rain or shine, work or no work, at the end of each week the money must be forthcoming."

Although "this was a hard bargain," men and women willingly accepted it whenever their masters and state laws permitted. For by backbreaking work —days, nights, Sundays, holidays—they could slowly scrape together the money to buy their liberty.

Charles White, a blacksmith in Virginia, hired his time for fifteen years until he had saved enough for "freedom papers." Aletheia Turner, who belonged to Thomas Jefferson, managed to buy herself in 1810. By 1828 she had bought her ten children, five grandchildren, and a sister. In the next ten years she freed two more women and their four children. A Georgia woman remained in slavery herself but used her earnings to purchase freedom for her five sons and daughters.

Even in the North former slaves devoted their lives to buying their families. A visitor to Cincinnati in 1834 "found one man who had just finished paying for his wife and five children. Another man and wife had bought themselves some years ago, and have been working day and night to purchase their children; they had just redeemed the last and had paid for themselves and children 1400 dollars! Another woman had recently paid the last installment of the purchase money for her husband. She had purchased him by taking in washing, and working late at night, after going out and performing as help at hard labor."

Only a few thousand slaves ever had the chance to win their liberty in this way. In the cotton fields and the sugar mills, where a man never saw a dollar from one end of the year to the other, he had to hunt for other ways to lighten his heavy load. Sometimes he had to be satisfied with a kind of freedom of the spirit, if only for an hour.

Master wanted work. He wanted cotton picked and corn planted and hogs fed. Master had whips and guns, police and patrollers. But the slave had himself. With a smiling face and a nodding head, he could misunderstand orders and take the longest time for the simplest task.

To prevent being driven beyond the limits of physical endurance, many slaves became "eye servants." They worked only when they were watched. "The overseer rode among them carrying in his hand a rawhide whip," a traveler in South Carolina reported. "As often as he visited one end of the line of operations, the hands at the other end would discontinue their labor." "They will never do more than just enough to save themselves from being punished," a Virginian agreed.

A cook in a South Carolina Big House won a small victory. "Alcey resolved that she would not cook any more. She systematically disobeyed orders and stole or destroyed the greater part of the provisions given to her for the table. Instead of getting the chickens for the dinner from the coop, she unearthed from some corner an old hen that had been setting for six weeks, and served her up as a fricassee! We had company to dinner that day; that would have deterred most of the servants, but not Alcey. She achieved her object, for she was sent to the field the next day."

Masters could never be sure whether a slave was ignorant or was deliberately sabotaging his work. "Let a hundred men shew him how to hoe, or drive a wheelbarrow, he'll still take the one by the Bottom and the other by the Wheel," a planter complained. "It always seems as if they took pains to break all the tools and spoil all the cattle that they possibly can," another said.

Careless slaves could forget to pour water on the coals over which they cooked, thereby setting fire to nearby barns and woods. There were so many plantation "accidents" that in 1820 the American Fire Insurance Company of Philadelphia refused "making insurances in any of the slave states."

On a Georgia plantation women were constantly "shamming themselves into the family-way in order to obtain a diminution of their labor," an overseer said. One mother-to-be enjoyed months of increased food rations "till she finally had to disappoint and receive a flogging." A slave who escaped work for years by pretending to be blind became "one of the best farmers in the country" after the Civil War.

Some of these "first-rate tricks to dodge work" show a grim determination. Slaves ate herbs from the woods, knowing that they would produce rashes and fever. A girl rubbed dirt into a cut to cause infection. A woman was given time off because of painful "swellings in her arms." It was weeks before her owner discovered that the swellings occurred when she plunged her arms into a beehive!

Even stories helped to remind the slave that, one way or another, he could still be his own man. Animal tales told by African ancestors took new forms in the cotton fields. Brother Rabbit, the most defenseless of all the animals, was always the hero. Brother Fox and Brother Lion might be bigger and stronger, but clever Brother Rabbit triumphed over them in the end. Another group of stories dealt directly with slave life. These were the tales of John, "a natural man," who matched wits with Old Master, the patrollers, and even the Devil. Sometimes John got into trouble, but more often than not his ready tongue saved him from punishment.

Above all, the slaves sang. Nonsense rhymes such as:

> I fooled Old Master seven years,
> Fooled the overseer three.
> Hand me down my banjo,
> And I'll tickle your bel-lee,

broke the dull routine of work in the fields. Sorrow songs and spirituals:

> Nobody knows the trouble I've seen,
> Nobody knows but Jesus,

or

> Swing low, sweet chariot,
> Coming for to carry me home.
> I looked over Jordan and what did I see?
> A band of angels coming after me,
> Coming for to carry me home,

offered still another way of escaping slavery's burdens.

Christianity came late to the "black and unknown bards" who composed this music. In Kamba's day most masters forbade the teaching of religion on their plantations. They were afraid that a Christian slave would consider himself the equal of his owner and demand his freedom. In 1800 only one slave in twenty-five was a church member. But as the cotton kingdom grew, Southern ministers began to read carefully selected Bible passages to prove that "God up in the sky had made black people to be slaves and white people to be masters."

A slave remembered these Sunday services. "He'd just say, 'Serve your masters. Don't steal your master's turkey. Don't steal your master's chickens. Don't steal your master's hogs. Do whatsoever your master tell you to do.' Same old thing all the time."

Although some Negroes accepted the idea that "God required them to wear their chains with meekness and humility," others who "could entertain no such nonsense" worked out their own version of Christianity. Slave preachers, black men who had somehow learned to read the Bible, told of a Jesus who had suffered oppression crueler than their own and a just God who led His people from bondage. Slaves dared not speak openly of freedom but they could sing:

> Didn't my Lord deliver Daniel
> And why not every man?
> He deliver'd Daniel from the lion's den,

> Jonah from the belly of the whale,
> And the Hebrew children from the fiery furnace,
> And why not every man?

or the challenging verses of:

> Go down, Moses,
> Way down in Egyptland.
> Tell old Pharaoh
> To let my people go.

After Nat Turner's rebellion, even these songs were banned. Like the early Christians in Rome, the slaves met secretly at night to worship God in their own way. Being caught at one of these "hush-harbor meetings" could mean a whipping, or worse.

"When we's coming back from that praying, I thunk I heared the Negro dogs and somebody on horseback. I say, 'Maw, it's them Negro hounds and they'll eat us up.' You could hear them old hounds a-baying. Maw listens and say, 'Sure 'nough, them dogs am running and God help us!' Then she and Paw take us to a fence corner and stands us up 'gainst the rails and say don't move. They went to the woods, so the hounds chase them and not git us. We hears the hounds come nearer. They goes after Paw and Maw, but they circles round to the cabins and gits in. Maw say it the power of God."

Sometimes a slave learned a patroller's plans and whispered a warning. "Patterollers is ridin' tonight. Watch out!" In the fields the warning was worked into a song:

Ain't gwine to be no meeting here tonight.
Don't you know, don't you know?
Creeks all muddy and the pond all dry.
Warn't for the tadpole, the fish all die.
So lie low, Lizzie, lie low.

In the Big House, where Mistress might overhear, the servants used double-talk. "Howdy, Mary," Jerry the footman said. "Did you know they was bugs in the wheat?" While Mistress raised an eyebrow over Jerry's nonsense Mary knew that "bugs" meant patrols and that she too must "lie low."

Even when the coast seemed clear, lookout boys were posted in nearby trees. Grapevines were stretched across the paths to trip the white men's horses and the slaves prayed with their heads bent over big iron pots which muffled the sound of their voices.

"We prays for the end of tribulations and the end of beatings and for shoes that fit our feet," a girl said. "We prayed that us Negroes could have all we wanted to eat and special for fresh meat."

But there were times when prayers alone could not comfort "a full heart and a troubled sperrit." At such a moment the slave who despaired of freedom ever coming to him might decide that he must go to freedom instead. Then, in the dead of night and at the risk of life, he ran away.

Freedom Ride

It was said long ago that the true romance of America was not in the fortunes of the Indian, nor in the New England character, nor in the social contrasts of Virginia planters, but in the story of the fugitive slave.

—Boston *Commonwealth*, 1863

RUNNING away was no longer so simple as it had been in the eighteenth century. The frontier forests were gone along the Atlantic seaboard. Steamboats puffed up the Western rivers and the Indian trails through the woods had become busy wagon roads. As cotton carried slavery south into Florida and across the Mississippi to Texas and Arkansas most fugitives turned toward the North.

It was a long lonely walk.

Charles Ball took it in 1810. A native of Maryland who had traveled in chains to Georgia, he determined to return to his wife and children. Preparing carefully for the trip, he repaired his boots and sewed a scabbard inside his coat so that he could carry a sword.

He filled a tin box with flints and tinder and a knapsack with bags of meal and parched corn. In August he was ready. In August a man could live on fruit and ripening corn.

Hiding in the woods during the day, he traveled at night with his eyes on the North Star. He ate peaches and roasted ears of corn. He got lost and was chased by patrollers and their dogs. Once he swam across an alligator-infested stream. Once he met a fugitive living in a lean-to made of tree boughs and for a few hours he feasted on stolen chicken and another man's company.

When November found him still in South Carolina, even the elements seemed against him. The leafless trees offered little concealment by day. At night clouds hid the North Star and he traveled in circles. Although he was close to populous settlements, he lived a Robinson Crusoe existence, making rough moccasins from a stolen hide when his boots wore out, catching an occasional possum or pig for supper. Most of the time he ate wild chestnuts and potatoes gleaned in the fields. He had no Man Friday to talk to.

On Christmas night it began to snow. Now there was the added danger that his footprints might be seen. Hungry, ragged, cold, he pushed on. Some nights he crossed ice-choked rivers. Some days he slept in deserted barns. March thaws made traveling easier, but the fields were bare of food and he had to steal oats from horses' troughs and parch them over his campfire.

Still Ball doggedly followed the North Star. With his heart in his throat, he walked boldly along the streets of Richmond on a Sunday afternoon in spring. Growing careless when he reached the familiar roads of Maryland, he was stopped by patrollers and thrown into jail. After thirty-nine days in a slave pen he managed to escape and travel the remaining miles to his wife's cabin. It was summer, 1811, when he was at last reunited with his family.

It would be nice to report that the Balls lived happily ever after. They almost did. Instead of turning him over to the authorities, his wife's master allowed him to share her cabin and work for wages in the neighborhood. Ball fought in the War of 1812, bought his own farm afterward, and lived free for twenty years. But in 1830 he was arrested as a fugitive and once more sold to a Georgia planter. This time he made short work of slavery. Running off to Savannah, he stowed away in the hold of a northbound ship. With the help of a Negro seaman he sailed to freedom.

Charles Ball's adventures were not extraordinary ones. One shoemaker from Virginia whose feet had been amputated when he was a boy made the long trek to Ohio walking on the stumps of his ankles. Another runaway sailed from a Southern port tied below the bowsprit of a steamer, half in, half out of icy salt water. A third, captured by bloodhounds who ripped his flesh and broke his arms, ran away again a year later, this time successfully.

Madison Washington lived up to his revolutionary name by organizing a rebellion on the brig *Creole* which was sailing from Richmond to New Orleans in 1841 with a cargo of tobacco and slaves. With belaying pins and capstan bars, the slaves took over the ship and forced the first mate to sail to Nassau, a British colony where slavery had been abolished some years before.

Mack was a light-skinned slave who had acquired the manners of a gentleman while traveling through Europe with his master. After their return he was sold to Black Jack Gamble, a slave trader whose complexion was swarthier than Mack's own. Gamble carried him off to New Orleans to sell him. When they met a planter who needed a field hand, Mack talked first. And smoothly. And persuasively. Gamble, he explained, was a capable worker although "so devilishly independent he thinks he is as good as a white man." Having sold his master, Mack proceeded to put on Gamble's best suit and book passage on a Mississippi River boat headed north!

Ellen, a lady's maid in Georgia, was also able to make use of her light skin. She was married to William Craft, a skilled cabinetmaker who hired his own time. Neither was badly treated but, said Ellen, "they would not give me my rights as a human being." To win these rights, the two planned to escape, with Ellen disguised as a young gentleman and William as her servant.

Dressed in men's clothes, her hair cropped short,

slender Ellen almost looked the part. Almost, but not quite. Something would have to be done about her beardless chin and high-pitched voice. Besides, how could she sign hotel registers when she didn't know how to write?

Night after night for more than a year they added bits to Ellen's disguise. A toothache obliged her to muffle her jaws with a scarf. Rheumatism provided an excuse for keeping her right arm in a sling. Deafness prevented her from talking. With green glasses and a cane to complete the transformation, Ellen became a planter's son on her way north for medical treatment.

Leaving the day after Christmas, when slaves were given an annual holiday, they traveled by steamship and train and stopped at the best hotels. Once they sat near a friend of Ellen's master, but her "deafness" prevented a conversation. Another time—it was in Baltimore on the last leg of their trip—a station agent refused William a ticket unless his owner posted a bond that was required of all Negroes going to the North. Hiding his dismay, glib William protested that delay might mean death for his delicate master. After a glance at the sickly young man, the agent pushed two tickets under his wicket and permitted the couple to board the train for Philadelphia.

Henry Brown had a shorter trip to make but he too made it in unusual style. It was a style that few travelers cared to imitate. A slave in Richmond, Virginia, Brown was five feet eight inches tall and weighed close to two hundred pounds. The statistics are important because in the winter of 1849 he built a packing case which was two feet wide, two and a half feet deep, and three feet long. When it was finished he curled up inside.

After supplying himself with a bladder of water, a handful of biscuits, and a gimlet to be used for boring holes in case he needed air, he asked Samuel Smith, a white friend, to nail down the lid. Smith addressed the box to a Philadelphia merchant known to be sympathetic to runaways, labeled it THIS SIDE UP and HANDLE WITH CARE and delivered it to the office of the Adams Express Company. From then on Henry Brown traveled as freight. He spent twenty-six hours, sometimes upended in spite of the labels, in the baggage cars.

For days beforehand mysterious messages had reached Philadelphia. A box *might* arrive on the 3 A.M. train from the South. The box *might* contain a man. These were followed at last by a telegram from Richmond: "Your case of goods is shipped and will arrive tomorrow morning."

Four worried gentlemen met to unpack the "case of goods." Would its contents be alive? With saw and hatchet they gingerly cut the hickory hoops that bound the box. As they pried off the lid, Henry Brown calmly reached out his hand and said, "Good morning, gentlemen." Uncurling his cramped legs, he stood up to sing the psalm that he had selected as his arrival hymn: "I waited patiently for the Lord, and He heard my prayer."

Eliza Harris arrived at the Kentucky shore of the Ohio River just as the thick winter ice was breaking up. With slave-catchers only minutes behind her, she tied her baby around her neck with a shawl and leaped from one ice cake to the next. Slipping to her knees, drenched by the icy water, she continued her flight until she reached Ohio.

Even today people all over the world know about Eliza's dramatic dash across the ice because Harriet Beecher Stowe told her story in *Uncle Tom's Cabin*. However, Eliza was only one of more than one hundred thousand slaves who walked, sailed, swam, or talked their way out of bondage in the half century before the Civil War. They stole boats and built rafts, using pieces of bark for paddles. They forged passes and bribed river men to hide them. They slept in cornfields, hollow trees, haystacks—and in the best front bedrooms of Ohio and Pennsylvania farmhouses. If their clothes wore out they dressed themselves in rabbit skins—or in garments that had been neatly stitched by Ladies' Aid societies.

Some, like Charles Ball, made their way to freedom alone, but others found hands stretched out to help them. While Eliza was racing across the icy Ohio with her baby a stranger waited for her on the north shore. He pulled her up the slippery riverbank and told her how to find the home of "a good man" who would give her dry clothes and shelter. The "good

man," living on a bluff overlooking the river where
Kentucky slaves could see his lamp at night, was a
conductor on the Underground Railroad.

The Underground Railroad acquired its name in
1831, some years before Eliza's escape. It was summer
and a slave swam across the Ohio while his master
rowed after him in a borrowed skiff. He had almost
caught up with him when the slave scrambled up the
bank and disappeared. No matter where the master
looked, no matter who he asked, he couldn't find the
runaway. Puzzled and angry, he returned to Kentucky declaring, "He must have gone on an underground road."

The men and women who sheltered runaways
chuckled over the Kentuckian's phrase—and improved
it. Steam trains chugging along on their iron rails were
the talk of the country that year. Why not an Underground Railroad which sped slaves to freedom? It
sounded mysterious and powerful.

Before the Revolution, respectable citizens had
gleefully donned war paint and feathers to dump a
load of tea into Boston Harbor. Now their descendants
protested against another injustice with the same kind
of fighting humor. The people who helped fugitive
slaves—and there were more and more of them as
time went on—spoke of themselves as "conductors,"
"stationmasters," "brakemen." They called their homes
"stations" or "depots" and they talked of "forward-
ing goods" and "catching the next train." When they

collected money for fugitives they were "selling stock in the road."

Levi Coffin, an Indiana Quaker, proudly claimed the title of President of the Underground Railroad because he helped more than three thousand slaves escape. So did Robert Purvis, a Philadelphia Negro who calculated that he had forwarded nine thousand runaways. Thomas Garrett, in the slave city of Wilmington, was close to the three-thousand mark in 1863 when, he jokingly complained, "the government went into the business and made a wholesale emancipation."

Despite their jokes, however, the Underground Railroad was a serious business. Even when a runaway reached a free state he was always in danger of capture. Armed slave-catchers, egged on by the promise of rewards, pursued him to Ohio and Pennsylvania, Boston and New York.

Stationmasters too ran risks. When Thomas Garrett was sixty years old he was given a heavy fine because he helped two children to escape. "Now that thee hast relieved me of what little I possessed," he told the judge, "I will go home and put another story on my house. I want room to accommodate more of God's poor." As the news of his trial reached plantations in Delaware and Maryland, so many slaves tapped on his windows at night that he did build an addition to his house to shelter them.

The Underground Railroad wasn't really a railroad, of course. Its tracks were country lanes, its lo-

comotives farm wagons and carriages, its conductors
ordinary people—Quakers, Yankees, free Negroes,
Presbyterians, Jews. A peddler built a false bottom
in his wagon. An undertaker loaned out his hearse.
A farmer dug a second cellar under his house, with
tunnels leading out to his barn and corncrib. A
housewife kept a kettle of water boiling on her stove
to threaten slave-catchers. A boy hitched up a team
and drove fugitives to the next station at night while
his father entertained their owner. There was even
a heroic horse named King William the Emancipator
and a wagon called The Liberator because it transported so many runaways.

Most Underground Railroad agents waited for
their passengers to appear, fed and clothed them,
and sent them on their way. They were obeying the
Bible, which said, "Thou shalt not deliver unto his
master the servant which is escaped." But increasingly, in the 1840s and '50s, men and women made
trips to the South. They called these "entering
Egypt" because they were helping slaves escape from
the land of bondage.

Handsome, reckless John Fairfield was a young
Virginian from a slaveholding family who devoted
his life to freeing slaves. Negroes in the North
brought him their savings and begged him to rescue
their families from the cotton fields. With his Southern accent and aristocratic manners, he could travel
through the slave states without arousing suspicion.

Often he rounded up dozens of slaves at one time

and spirited them away. Once when he discovered that a number of his "clients" in Maryland, Virginia, and Washington, D.C., were light-skinned, he invested his expense money in theatrical make-up. Assembling his Maryland passengers in Baltimore, he helped them put on wigs and apply powder and paint to their faces. Then he sent them by train to Harrisburg, Pennsylvania. Similarly wigged and powdered, a second group of slaves rode the cars from Washington to Pittsburgh.

By the time Fairfield set out from Virginia with his third set of passengers, slaveowners had learned of his strategy. While he traveled north in the Pittsburgh express, they hired a special train and raced after him. With a full head of steam and a clear track, they were pulling abreast of the express as it neared Pittsburgh. As the brakeman slowed down for the stop, Fairfield hustled his freedom riders from their seats. With wigs aslant and mufflers flying, they jumped from the train steps and scattered through the city. They were never caught.

Most of the conductors who ventured into the South were Negroes. From Virginia, "Ham & Eggs" regularly transported "very good hams" to Pennsylvania stations. Jane Lewis rowed fugitives across the Ohio at night. Josiah Henson, Harriet Beecher Stowe's model for Uncle Tom, commuted between Canada and Kentucky, leading out more than one hundred slaves.

The best-known conductor was Harriet Tubman,

called "Moses" on every plantation in the South. A woman close to thirty when she escaped, short of stature, subject to sudden sleeping spells, unable to write her name, she "entered Egypt" nineteen times. With a $4000 reward—dead or alive—hanging over her head, she rescued three hundred slaves.

Wearing simple disguises—a floppy sunbonnet or a man's old hat—she would sing as she plodded along the dark country roads at night:

> "When that old chariot comes,
> Who's going with me?"

Informed by the grapevine of her arrival, a slave would reply:

> "When that old chariot comes,
> I'm going with you."

Usually her "train" departed on a Saturday night so that it would have a day's start before its passengers were missed. Once under way, there was no turning back on Harriet's road. The ticking bag around her waist contained medicine for the sick, food for the hungry—and a pistol for the faint of heart. If a man was exhausted, she would ford a stream, carrying him in her arms. But if it was fear that made him falter, her trigger finger tightened and she ordered him to "Move or die!"

Traveling on foot, she financed most of her trips by her earnings as a cook. After she had freed brothers, sisters, nieces, nephews, and a host of friends she determined to rescue her aged parents. Because they were unable to walk long distances, she brought them away "in a singular manner," Thomas Garrett recalled. "They started with an old horse, fitted out in primitive style with a straw collar, a pair of old chaise wheels, with a board on the axle to sit on, another board swing with ropes to rest their feet on. She got her parents on this rude vehicle and drove to town in a style that no human being ever did before or since. Next day, I furnished her with money to take them all to Canada."

Asked to speak at a women's rights meeting in upstate New York, Harriet's sharp eyes twinkled as she rose to her introduction. "Yes, ladies," she said, "I can say what most conductors can't—I never ran my train off the track and I never lost a passenger."

A Man and a Brother

Has the God who made the white man and the black left any record declaring us a different species? Are we not supported by the same food, hurt by the same wounds, pleased with the same delights? And should we not then enjoy the same liberty, and be protected by the same laws?
—JAMES FORTEN, 1813

AT A meeting on the island of Nantucket in 1841 a tall young man with a shock of wavy hair rose to say a few words. Less than three years out of slavery, he was shaking with stage fright. This was the first time he had addressed a white audience. But when he talked of his childhood and youth as a slave the words came tumbling out. His listeners sat on the edges of their seats, blew their noses, or openly wept.

In the silence that followed his speech, abolitionist William Lloyd Garrison stepped forward. "Have we been listening to a thing, a piece of property, or to a man?" he asked.

"A man! A man!" five hundred voices shouted.

"And should such a man be held a slave in a republican and Christian land?"

"No, no! Never!"

"Should such a man ever be sent back to slavery?"

The audience roared "No!" until the walls of the building seemed to bulge. The men and women who were present remembered that afternoon on Nantucket Island all their lives. "I think I never hated slavery so intensely," Garrison said. "There stood one in physical proportions and stature, commanding, in intellect, richly endowed, in natural eloquence, a prodigy—yet a fugitive slave, trembling for his safety."

The new name on the roll call of runaways was Frederick Douglass. When he was a boy of eight, working as a servant in Baltimore, a kind mistress taught him the letters of the alphabet. Taught him until her husband ripped the book from her hand and stormed, "Learning will spoil the best Negro in the world. If you teach him how to read, he'll want to know how to write, and this accomplished he'll be running away with himself."

This was all the boy needed to hear. From then on he stole his learning. He spelled out chalked words on sidewalks and fences, copied the initials written on timber at the shipyards, rescued scraps of paper from street gutters.

When he listened to guests attacking "the abolitionists" he searched for the word in his master's dictionary. "The dictionary offered me very little help," he recalled in after years. "It taught me that abolition was 'the act of abolishing,' but it left me in ignorance as to the thing to be abolished." Not until he painfully read through a newspaper did he discover that "the thing to be abolished" was slavery.

It was a lesson he never forgot. Twice he made plans to run away. When the second attempt succeeded, he settled in New Bedford, Massachusetts. Finding work in the shipyards there, he married and had children. He had been in the North only a few months when he started attending abolitionist meetings. On his first vacation he sailed to Nantucket to attend an anti-slavery convention. Before the convention adjourned he had been asked to become a lecturer for the Massachusetts Anti-Slavery Society.

For the next twenty years Douglass spoke day and night, at gatherings in the Northern states and in England. At first he was the abolitionists' prize exhibit. He was a slave who had freed himself, like the Crafts and Henry "Box" Brown with whom he sometimes shared a platform. "Many persons in the audience could not believe that he was actually a slave," a reporter wrote. "How a man who had never gone to school a day in his life, could speak with such eloquence—with such precision of language and power of thought—they were utterly at a loss to devise."

Douglass quickly became the leader and spokesman for the Negro people in the United States. Au-

thor of a best-selling autobiography, he edited his
own newspaper, the *North Star*, until after the
Emancipation Proclamation was signed. During the
Civil War he was invited to the White House to
counsel the President on the employment of Negro
troops.

Douglass was not the first man of his race to tell
the world about "the thing to be abolished." In Philadelphia, freeborn James Forten wrote anti-slavery
pamphlets as early as 1813. After serving as a powder boy on the *Royal Louis* during the Revolution,
Forten invented a machine for handling sails that
earned him a fortune. Although Pennsylvania law
forbade him to vote because of his color, he consci-
entiously shepherded his white employees to the
polls each Election Day. The Reverend Richard Allen, who had bought himself from his master, joined
Forten in protesting a plan to send free Negroes to
Africa. Allen founded the African Methodist Episcopal
Church after an usher in a "white" house of worship
pulled him from his knees while he was praying.

In New York in 1827 brown-skinned Samuel Cor-
nish and John Russworm started *Freedom's Journal*,
the country's first Negro newspaper. In Boston two
years later David Walker published an "Appeal to
the Coloured Citizens of the World," calling on the
slaves to rebel, while George Moses Horton, a North
Carolina slave, wrote poems "On Liberty and Slavery."

Despite these activities, the abolition societies

formed at the time of the Revolution were virtually
out of business during the first decades of the nineteenth century. They had been founded in the belief
that slavery was dying out. When it grew stronger,
instead, the societies frankly admitted that they
didn't know what to do. One of the few white abolitionists who continued to speak against slavery was
Benjamin Lundy. A Quaker, Lundy published, edited, and wrote the *Genius of Universal Emancipation*. Hiking across the country with his type in a
pack on his back, he stopped wherever he could find
a press to use, printed an issue of his paper and
moved on.

When he hired a young assistant named William
Lloyd Garrison things began to hum. Garrison believed that the slaves should be freed immediately,
not at some vague distant date. In spite of protests
from Lundy's readers, he said so at every opportunity. After spending seven weeks in a Baltimore jail
because he called New England shipowners who
transported slaves "highway robbers and murder-
ers," he parted company with the soft-voiced Lundy.
In 1831—the year that saw Nat Turner's rebellion
and the naming of the Underground Railroad—he
went to Boston to start a paper of his own, the *Liberator*.

"I will be as harsh as truth and as uncompromising
as justice," he wrote in his first issue. "On this subject, I do not wish to think, or speak, or write, with
moderation. No! No! Tell a man whose house is on

fire to give a moderate alarm . . . tell the mother to gradually extricate her babe from the fire into which it has fallen;—but urge me not to use moderation in a cause like the present. I am in earnest—I will not equivocate—I will not excuse—I will not retreat a single inch—*and I will be heard.*"

The twenty-six-year-old printer from Massachusetts was a most unlikely-looking warrior. Something of a dandy in his dress, he was prematurely bald, with silver-rimmed spectacles that hid near-sighted eyes. People meeting him for the first time were surprised to find him "so mild and meek." But when he had a stick of type in his hand he could be merciless.

The front page of the *Liberator* carried a drawing of a slave auction near the Capitol in Washington. Its columns were filled with scorching editorial attacks on slavery. Garrison minced no words in describing slaveowners as "man-stealers" or "kidnapers." He was equally severe with their Northern defenders. To show the cruelty of the slave system, he reprinted without comment advertisements describing runaway slaves: "He had one ear cropped off and his back was badly cut up" or "Had on each foot an iron ring with a small chain attached to it."

The *Liberator* was noisy, righteous, angry—and it was heard. Garrison's first readers were mostly Negroes. He might never have been able to publish if James Forten, the Philadelphia sailmaker, had not sent him money and sold subscriptions for him. But the paper's hard-hitting style soon made others stop, think, and decide to do something about slavery. In 1833 sixty men traveled to Philadelphia to form the American Anti-Slavery Society.

"More than fifty-seven years have elapsed since a band of patriots convened in this place, to devise measures for the deliverance of this country from a foreign yoke," their Declaration of Sentiments proclaimed. "We have met together for the achievement of an enterprise, without which, that of our fathers is incomplete. We believe and affirm that the slaves ought instantly to be set free and brought under the protection of law."

Most of the group were Quakers or "peace men" who were opposed to violence. They didn't believe in organizing slave rebellions. They planned to appeal to the conscience of the nation by debating, preaching, writing, meeting. They saw their cause as a holy crusade, to be waged with "Prayer, Faith, and the word of God."

The next years were ones of mounting excitement. Anti-slavery societies were formed in every state in the North until there were two thousand societies with more than two hundred thousand members. Traveling lecturers held meetings in churches and halls—and in stables and barns when public buildings were forbidden to them. Once when Frederick Douglass could find no place to hold a meeting he borrowed a dinner bell. Ringing the bell as he walked along the main streets of the town, he called out: "Notice! Frederick Douglass, recently a slave, will lecture on American slavery on Grafton Common this evening at seven o'clock!"

Anti-slavery lecturers included not only ex-slaves but ex-slaveowners like James Birney of Alabama and Angelina Grimke of South Carolina. Many of the speakers were students from Lane Seminary in Cincinnati and Oberlin College in Ohio, which had just opened its doors to Negroes and to women.

A host of new publications appeared: the *Anti-Slavery Standard*, the *Anti-Slavery Bugle*, *Anti-Slavery Record*, *Emancipator*, *Herald of Freedom*. There was even a magazine for children called the *Slave's Friend*. Alongside these were mountains of pamphlets—"American Slavery as It Is," "An Appeal in Favor of That Class of Americans Called Africans," "Human Rights"—which were sent through the mails or left on doorsteps.

The abolitionist movement involved every member of the family. Women who had been permitted to attend the 1833 convention, but not of course to sign the Declaration, formed Female Societies. They knitted stockings and sewed shirts for runaway slaves. They used tea parties and social calls to obtain signatures on anti-slavery petitions and to distribute anti-slavery publications. Then they held bazaars and fairs to raise money for more petitions and more pamphlets. Some women even began to speak against slavery in public, to the horror of most men.

While their daughters crocheted on samplers,

"May the point of our needles prick the slaveholders' consciences," their sons, with some prodding perhaps, turned down candy and cake made from Louisiana sugar. Maple sugar and honey-flavored cookies might not taste as good, but the paper in which they were wrapped said:

> Take this, my friend, you need not fear to eat,
> No slave has toiled to cultivate this sweet.

Several cities boasted of Free Produce Stores which sold "free" cloth, manufactured from cotton grown by Quakers who owned no slaves. "Free calicoes could seldom be called handsome, free umbrellas were hideous to look upon," one girl complained. But, said her elders, "the sighs of the brokenhearted will not linger among their folds."

Young abolitionists found their reward at the anti-slavery fairs and festivals. There was always a picnic on August 1, to celebrate the anniversary of emancipation in the British West Indies, and a fair before Christmas where gifts could be bought "and a benevolent cause thus aided without any extra outlay of money."

After the speeches were over, everyone unbent at these affairs and Garrison delighted the young people with puns and stories. Describing a fair in Boston, James Russell Lowell wrote:

> There's Garrison, his features very
> Benign for an incendiary,
> Beaming forth sunshine through his glasses
> On the surrounding lads and lasses.

Even Quaker youngsters whose elders frowned on music joined in the choruses when the Hutchinson family, known as the Singing Yankees, led the audience in a hymn that Garrison had written:

> "I am an Abolitionist,
> I glory in the name"

or sang:

> "Ho! The car Emancipation
> Rides majestic thro' our Nation,
> Bearing on its train the story,
> Liberty! a nation's glory."

As a result of all this outpouring of energy, tens of thousands of people came to hate slavery with a deep personal hatred. They also began to know their Negro fellow citizens. Men with dark skins had signed the original Declaration of Sentiments of the Anti-Slavery Society and had served on its first board of managers. Their wives were members of the Female Societies. Their children attended the bazaars and picnics.

After listening to speakers like Frederick Douglass, few could swallow the South's picture of slaves as "the happiest human beings on whom the sun shines" or believe that they were "naturally inferior" to whites. Nor could they continue to think of Negroes only as objects of pity—"miserable wretches," "God's poor"—to be helped out of the charity that welled up in good men's hearts.

Sitting alongside Negroes at meetings and visiting

their homes, white abolitionists discovered that even in the North they were unfairly treated. Their children were not allowed to attend public schools. They could seldom ride on trains or omnibuses except in dirty "Jim Crow" cars. Most theaters and concerts were forbidden to them and even churches had special "Negro pews."

Abolitionists began to fight against these restrictions, petitioning school committees and suing in the courts until schoolrooms were opened to Negro pupils. They boycotted busses which refused to carry Negro passengers. When Frederick Douglass was not allowed to enter a stateroom on a steamer, but was ordered instead to the forward deck where horses and sheep were quartered, his white companion joined him. "I could not persuade him," Douglass said, "to leave me to bear the burden of insult and outrage alone."

This change in attitude didn't come about overnight. For a long time neither group was sure how to act toward the other. When Richard Henry Dana, author of *Two Years before the Mast*, visited an abolitionist's home he was surprised to be introduced to Negroes "by their surnames with the prefixes of Mr. and Mrs. He introduced us to them in due form, 'Mr. Dana, Mr. Jefferson; Mrs. Metcalf, Mrs. Wait.' It was plain they had never been so treated or spoken to before and what to do on the introduction was quite beyond their experience."

A well-known Boston doctor who was interested

in a young lady who disliked abolitionists told of meeting Frederick Douglass. "As I would have invited a white friend, I asked him home to dine with me. It is useless to deny that I did not like the thought of walking with him in open midday up Washington Street. I *hoped* I would not meet any of my acquaintances. I had, however, hardly turned into the street before I met the young lady. I am glad now to say that I *did not skulk.* I looked at her straight and bowed in 'my most gracious manner' as if I were 'all right' while I saw by her look of great regret that she thought me 'all wrong.' It was, however, something like a cold sponge-bath—that Washington Street walk by the side of a black man—rather terrible at the outset, but wonderfully warming and refreshing afterwards!"

There were many ways to arouse the conscience of a nation. Not the least of them, in 1841, was to take a walk up Washington Street with a new friend. For the first time since Portuguese and Spanish ships explored the African coast, some white men and women were beginning to answer the Negroes' question, "AM I NOT A MAN AND A BROTHER?" with a clear-cut "YES."

The Cotton Curtain

I think we must get rid of slavery, or we must get rid of freedom.

—RALPH WALDO EMERSON

As SOON as the anti-slavery crusade got under way slaveowners hastened to seal off the South from the rest of the country. The written word of the abolitionists was outlawed. Otherwise it might encourage the ordinary people of the South—small farmers and tradesmen who owned no slaves—to oppose the slave system.

The first target was the *Liberator*. The weekly was only two months old when Georgia's legislature offered $4000 for Garrison's arrest. South Carolina called on the mayor of Boston to suppress the paper and posted a $1500 reward for anyone caught distributing it. One Georgia subscriber was tarred and feathered, burned, ducked in the river, and whipped.

Even an ardent abolitionist might cancel his subscription after that treatment!

The ban quickly spread to all anti-slavery publications. The penalty for circulating these was twenty years in jail in Maryland, life imprisonment in Louisiana. Virginia, Tennessee, and Alabama passed similar laws, Alabama's statute forbidding not only newspapers but anything written on wood, cloth, metal, or stone. School texts from the North were carefully examined. One dusty old history book was found to contain "hidden lessons of the most fiendish and murderous character that enraged fanaticism could conceive."

After Charleston's *Southern Patriot* reported the arrival of a ship from New York with anti-slavery mail, a mob broke into the post office, seized and burned the letters. The postmaster, who disliked mobs cluttering up his post office, called on Washington for help, but the Postmaster General, a slaveholder, advised him not to worry. "We have an obligation to the laws," he wrote, "but we owe a higher one to the communities in which we live."

The conscientious Charlestonian pursued the matter further. He asked the postmaster in New York to hold up anti-slavery mailings and the New Yorker obligingly did so. Soon afterward President Jackson proposed a federal law banning "incendiary publications" in the South. The law failed to pass but postmasters everywhere set themselves up as censors.

The wall around the Southern states grew higher and higher. "Thou shalt not read about slavery" was joined by "Thou shalt not speak." A Virginian who said that "black men have, in the abstract, a right to their freedom" was whipped and ridden out of town on a rail. A North Carolina preacher spent a winter in jail for questioning slavery. A Louisiana minister was hanged in effigy and a Bible salesman suspected of abolitionist sentiments was lashed in the square of a Tennessee town. A college professor rumored to have voted for the "wrong" candidate lost his job and fled for his life while three men were killed in Georgia and South Carolina for the crime of "association with Negroes."

"The expression of any sentiment at all conflicting with the gospel of slavery, dooms them at once, and then they are obliged to become heroes, martyrs, or exiles," a North Carolinian wrote—after he had left home.

Only in the border states were there occasional cracks in the wall. Cassius Clay managed to publish an anti-slavery paper in Kentucky, in a building protected by sheet iron and defended by two brass cannon. After a time, however, slaveowners, unceremoniously moved Clay's press across the river to Cincinnati.

Even the free North was far from free. Except for the abolitionists, most people didn't care one way or another about Negroes or slavery. Some workmen feared that large numbers of freed slaves might endanger their jobs. Many businessmen had ties with the South that they didn't want broken.

"There are millions upon millions of dollars due from Southerners to the merchants and mechanics of this city," a New Yorker told a friend of Garrison's. "We cannot afford, sir, to let you and your associates succeed in your endeavor to overthrow slavery. It is not a matter of principle with us. It is a matter of business necessity. We mean, sir, to put you abolitionists down—by fair means if we can, by foul means if we must."

While the South was clapping its hands to its ears, a substantial number of Northerners used theirs to toss rotten eggs and ripe tomatoes at abolitionist speakers. John Greenleaf Whittier cheerfully preserved his egg-stained coat as a souvenir of his speaking engagements. "Stones and clubs flew merrily against the shutters," Theodore Weld reported after lecturing in Ohio. "Nails, divers pockets full of stones and eggs had been provided for the occasion."

James Russell Lowell composed a poem about Stephen Foster, another abolitionist speaker:

> Hard by, as calm as summer even,
> Smiles the reviled and pelted Stephen;
> Who studied mineralogy
> Not with soft book upon the knee,
> But learned the properties of stones,
> By contact sharp of flesh and bones.

Despite their attempts to laugh off these attacks, many were deadly serious. In Boston a well-dressed mob dragged William Lloyd Garrison through the streets with a rope around his waist. "The plan," he was later told, "was to take you to the Common, strip, tar-and-feather you, and then dye your face and hands black in a manner that would never change from a night Negro color." Rescued by the mayor, Garrison was then arrested for causing a riot.

When Prudence Crandall, a Quaker schoolteacher in Connecticut, accepted a Negro pupil she lived through a two-year reign of terror. Merchants refused to sell her food. Doctors wouldn't treat sick students. Rocks were thrown through windows and manure poisoned the school well. In a school assembly four of her students sang:

> "Sometimes when we have walked the streets
> Saluted we have been,
> By guns and drums and cow bells too
> And horns of polished tin.
>
> With warnings, threats, and words severe
> They visit us at times,
> And gladly would they send us off
> To Afric's burning climes."

Miss Crandall didn't give up until a group of her neighbors set fire to her school and used clubs and iron bars to wreck the classrooms.

After two Negro boys entered Noyes Academy in New Hampshire, citizens assembling at a town meeting acted quickly. They tied ropes around the school building one night, hitched up a hundred yoke of oxen and, with a mighty heave, hauled the school away to a nearby swamp.

Homes and churches were burned, Negroes stoned and beaten in New York and Utica. Anti-abolitionists in Cincinnati destroyed the press which printed James Birney's *Philanthropist*. Philadelphians burned down Pennsylvania Hall during an abolitionist convention there. "In the heart of this city a flame has gone up to Heaven," Whittier wrote. "In its red and lurid light, men will see more clearly by what a frail tenure they hold property and life in a land overshadowed by the curse of slavery."

The tide began to turn when Elijah Lovejoy, a minister from Maine, started an anti-slavery newspaper in southern Illinois. Three times the citizens of Alton dumped his press into the Mississippi River. When a fourth press arrived, his friends armed themselves to defend it. During a pitched battle Lovejoy fell to the ground with five bullets through his chest.

Lovejoy's death shocked the country, bringing more recruits to the anti-slavery cause than a thousand meetings had done. When the Illinois legislature passed a resolution attacking abolitionists and defending slavery, thirty-year-old Abraham Lincoln was one of two members who voted against it. He was troubled, he told the Young Men's Lyceum in Springfield, by the "outrages committed by mobs from New England to Louisiana." If men are permitted to "throw printing-presses into rivers, shoot editors, and hang and burn obnoxious persons at pleasure and with impunity, depend upon it, this government cannot last."

Another young man elbowed his way through the crowd in Faneuil Hall in Boston to point out that American liberties were in danger. His first public speech "electrified the mighty assembly," a Boston newspaper wrote. From that day on, handsome well-born Wendell Phillips gave up the practice of law to take his place alongside Garrison and Douglass as the abolitionists' most eloquent speaker.

A sheepherder with the undistinguished name of John Brown attended a memorial meeting for Love-joy in Ohio. When the speeches were over he raised his right hand and swore to devote his life to the destruction of slavery. He too would be heard from again.

In Washington, Congress itself was becoming a battleground. The District of Columbia was one of the country's busiest slave markets. Almost any morning, shocked foreign diplomats could stand on the Capitol steps and watch groups of slaves trudge along Pennsylvania Avenue in chains. Since the first years of the Republic, abolitionist groups had petitioned Congress to end slavery in the District. These petitions had been referred to a committee, forgotten, or denied.

With the growth of anti-slavery societies, petitions against slavery in Washington began to pour in. Alarmed by their numbers, Southern congressmen decided to deal with them in a new way. In 1836

the House of Representatives passed a resolution
known as the "gag rule." This provided that all petitions concerning slavery be "laid on the table" without being read. The subject of slavery in the country's capital was closed. Period.

The gag rule was something the abolitionists
could get their teeth into. District by district, city
by city, state by state, they organized the North and
collected signatures. One "immense roll of paper"
from Boston was "about the size of an ordinary barrel." A Massachusetts county gathered 200,000
names in a single year. Bundles of petitions arrived
in Washington by every train. Bales of them were delivered to the House. Millions of people signed them.

Seventy-year-old John Quincy Adams, former
President of the United States and son of the first
John Adams, became the petitioners' champion.
Along with many of the signers of the petitions, he
disapproved of the fiery abolitionists. He was even
opposed to emancipation in the District. But he believed strongly in the American Bill of Rights. While
the Speaker banged his gavel and his colleagues
howled "Order!" Adams used one parliamentary
trick after another to force the House to hear him.

Session after session, he read petitions against slavery, petitions opposing the annexation of Texas, and
even a petition from Virginia asking that John Quincy
Adams be expelled from Congress. Once he kept the
House in an uproar for three days by threatening to
read a petition from a group of slaves. When he fi-

nally won the floor he solemnly read their request to be protected from abolitionist agitators. It was, said one historian, "the most effective practical joke in the history of Congress."

As his lonely battle made headlines, a handful of anti-slavery men from New England and Ohio were elected to join him. Most of them lived at the same boardinghouse near the Capitol. Their landlady was careful to hire only free Negroes as servants, because slaves who waited on these congressmen had a habit of booking passage on the Underground Railroad.

Adams and the anti-slavery men won at last. The gag rule was abandoned in 1844. It had taken eight years but it taught the country a useful lesson. All over the North men were beginning to believe that liberty for the white man could not be secure without liberty for the slave.

The Darkening Sky

*We Americans are very fond of this glue of com-
promise. Like so many quack cements, it is advertised to make the mended parts of the vessel
stronger than those which have never been broken,
but like them it will not stand hot water.*
                                   —JAMES RUSSELL LOWELL

THE struggle to end the gag rule was part of
a larger struggle for control of the United States.
The annexation of Texas and war with Mexico were
opening up vast new lands. The Republic's borders
now stretched south to the Rio Grande and west to
the Pacific Ocean. Gold was being mined in California and there was talk of a railroad that would
span the continent. Thousands of immigrants were arriving every month from Europe, to find factory jobs
or homesteads on the Great Plains.

Would the industrial North or the planter South
dominate these rich new territories? Someday it
would have to be one or the other, for, as Wendell
Phillips said, "You cannot make a nation one half

steamboats, sewing machines and Bibles, and the other half slaves."

Two thirds of the country's population and a still larger share of its wealth belonged to the North. But the abolitionists were only a minority. Their neighbors might think that slavery was wrong, but they were willing to let the Southern states decide the issue for themselves. The new territories, however, were another matter. By the middle of the nineteenth century, most Northerners agreed that the territories should be free.

The South was unified. Their leaders believed not only that slavery was right but that it was necessary for their survival. By voting as a bloc and bringing pressure on Northerners who did business with them, they had been able to control Congress, the President, and even the Supreme Court, for many years. Frightened by the growing sentiment against slavery, they were more determined than ever to win new land for their cotton kingdom.

Whenever a disagreement on national policy arose in Congress, Southern spokesmen threatened to leave the Union. Then worried statesmen from both sections would step forward to propose a compromise. Starting with the first compromises at the Constitutional Convention, the South had always gotten the best of the bargains. Horace Greeley, editor of the New York *Tribune*, described these victories:

"'Buy Louisiana for us!' said the slaveholders. 'With Pleasure.' 'Now Florida!' 'Certainly.' 'Next: Violate your treaties with the Creeks and Cherokees so as to let us expand our plantations.' 'So said, so done.' 'Now for Texas!' 'You have it.' 'Next, a third more of Mexico!' 'Yours it is.' 'Now, break the Missouri Compact, and let Slavery wrestle with Free Labor for the vast region consecrated by that Compact to Freedom!' 'Very good. What next?'"

What next? A struggle in Congress lasting for almost a year resulted in the Compromise of 1850. In return for the admission of California as a free state and the end of the slave trade—but not slavery—in the District of Columbia, slaveholders were to be protected against the loss of their slave property by a harsh new Fugitive Slave Law.

Neither section was pleased with the bargain. While Georgia, Alabama, Mississippi, and South Carolina talked of secession, Northerners were shocked by the Fugitive Slave Law. Under its provisions, any Negro living in the North could be carried off to slavery, if a slaveowner appeared before a federal commissioner and claimed him as his property. The man with a dark skin was allowed no defense, no witness to testify for him, no jury trial, no appeal. Moreover, the commissioner hearing the case was given a ten-dollar fee if he decided in favor of the slaveowner and only five dollars if he set the Negro free. The new law obligated every citizen to help catch runaways. If he refused, or actually aided the fugitives, he could be fined and sent to jail.

President Fillmore's signature on the law was

scarcely dry when two men from Macon, Georgia, registered at the United States Hotel in Boston. They carried warrants for the arrest of William and Ellen Craft.

A newly formed Vigilance Committee immediately went into action. Ellen was spirited away from her job in an upholsterer's shop and hidden outside the city. William left his carpenter's bench for the well-guarded home of Lewis Hayden, another exslave. With armed men posted at the doors, Hayden sat in the basement alongside kegs of gunpowder. He was prepared to blow up his house if a marshal set foot in it.

Meanwhile, white members of the Vigilance Committee trailed the Georgians. Whenever they left their hotel, crowds gathered on the streets to shout, "Slave hunters—there go the slave hunters!" After five days in the city they were still unable to find a commissioner who would hear their case although "I'll have them," one swore, "if I have to stay here to all eternity."

When it was rumored that federal troops were on their way to Massachusetts to enforce the law, sixty Bostonians paid a formal call on the slave-catchers. Arriving at six o'clock in the morning, they calmly seated themselves on the hotel's staircase, while their leaders rapped on the Georgians' door. A sober look at the visitors convinced the pair that it would be healthier to take the next train to New York.

The opponents of the Fugitive Slave Law had won

the first round, but this was only the beginning. The Crafts fled to England, their passage paid by Boston friends. They didn't dare to return home until after the Civil War. Thousands of other ex-slaves who had been living peacefully in the North packed up their belongings and headed for the long bridge crossing the Niagara River into Canada. Whole communities in Pennsylvania and upstate New York disappeared overnight.

"The anguish, the terror, the agony inflicted by this infamous statute, must be witnessed to be fully appreciated," said William Still, secretary of Philadelphia's Vigilance Committee. "You must hear the tale of the broken-hearted mother, who has just received tidings that her son is in the hands of man-thieves. You must listen to the impassioned appeal of the wife whose husband's retreat has been discovered. You must hear the husband beg you for God's sake to save his wife."

Like the Minute Men of an earlier day, Vigilance Committees ready to ride and spread the alarm formed in New York, Chicago, Detroit, Milwaukee. Courthouse and church bells were rung and streets echoed with "Freemen! To the rescue! The man-hunters are in the land."

The Vigilance men were lawyers, doctors, writers, ministers, merchants. They put aside their beliefs in non-violence and talked of a "higher law." The Reverend Theodore Parker, who led Boston's sit-in against the two Georgia slave hunters, wrote his sermons "with a sword in the open drawer under my ink-stand, and a pistol in the flap of the desk, loaded and ready for defense."

"The Stamp Act could not be executed here. Can the Fugitive Slave Bill?" Senator Charles Sumner asked. "I will not obey it, by God," Ralph Waldo Emerson swore.

In the years following the Compromise, many fugitives were rescued. An ex-slave known as Shadrach was hustled from a Boston courtroom by a crowd of Negroes. Abolitionists meeting in Syracuse took Jerry McHenry from a prison cell and spirited him off to Canada. Charles Nalle was rescued from a United States marshal in Troy. In Chicago a fugitive jumped through a courtroom window to freedom. In Milwaukee five thousand men assembled in front of the jail. With a wooden beam on their shoulders, they battered down the door and carried Joshua Glover to the nearest Underground Railroad station.

Even when a runaway was sent back to slavery, the defeat sometimes turned into victory. In 1854 the whole country watched when a federal commissioner ordered the return of Anthony Burns from Boston to Virginia. After one rescue attempt failed, the President and governor ordered out two thousand soldiers—artillery, infantry, marines—to guard the streets.

It was a cloudless day in June when Burns was marched from the courthouse to Long Wharf where a revenue cutter waited for him. Church bells tolled and buildings along the line of march were draped in mourning. Opposite the State House a coffin labeled "The Funeral of Liberty" hung from a window. Fifty thousand spectators who had come from all over the state hissed and groaned and shouted, "Shame!"

Watching from his office, one lawyer said, "I put my face in my hands and wept. I could do nothing less."

"There was a lot of folks to see a colored man walk down the street," Anthony Burns dryly commented.

After four months spent in handcuffs in a slave jail in Richmond, he was ransomed by Negro and white friends, who raised $1300 to buy him from his master. He turned down P. T. Barnum's offer of an engagement at Barnum's Museum because "He wants to show me like a monkey." Instead he accepted a scholarship to Oberlin College. Ordained as a Baptist minister, he later joined a settlement of former slaves in Canada.

INCUR ANY EXPENSE, President Pierce had wired the United States marshal in Boston. But the cost ran far higher than the $100,000 spent for troops and revenue cutter. The Burns case boomeranged. The startling display of federal force lined up against one frightened fugitive disturbed drowsing consciences. One after another, Northern states passed personal-liberty laws that made the Fugitive Slave Law difficult to enforce. No other runaway was ever captured on Massachusetts soil.

"A few more such victories and the South is undone," the Richmond *Enquirer* said.

In the same month that Anthony Burns was returned to slavery the Kansas-Nebraska Act became a law. For more than thirty years Congress had agreed that territories north of the 36°30′ latitude line would be free when they entered the Union. Throwing out the old Compromise, the new act said that it was up to the inhabitants of the two territories to decide whether to become free or slave states. Only there weren't any inhabitants of Kansas and Nebraska—or at least not any who could vote. Only buffalo and Indians and an occasional fur trader roamed the Great Plains. When the passage of the act offered a chance to "vote slavery up or down" in an area larger than the original thirteen colonies, there was a sudden scramble for the prairie lands.

The Southerners got there first. With fast horses, Missourians could ride across the border, cast ballots, and be home again the same day. Anyone was an "inhabitant," they declared, who arrived in Kansas on Election Day. Particularly if he slung his rifle across his saddle and carried a bowie knife in his jeans.

It was harder for Easterners who planned real settlements. Crossing half a continent with their wives and children, they needed shelter against the bitter Kansas winter and food to tide them over until harvest time. Leading citizens of Massachusetts formed

an Emigrant Aid Society to give these Kansas colonists a grubstake in their first hard years and to build
hotels, gristmills, and schools. When twenty-four
men and women left Boston for Kansas in the summer of 1854, John Greenleaf Whittier wrote a song
for them:

> We cross the prairie as of old
> The pilgrims crossed the sea,
> To make the West, as they the East
> The homestead of the free!
>
> We go to rear a wall of men
> On Freedom's southern line
> And plant beside the cotton-tree
> The rugged Northern pine!

By fall the colonists had built log houses with sod-
covered roofs and were staking out farms. Their first
town was named Lawrence, after Amos Lawrence,
one of New England's wealthiest mill owners. He
hoped to make money from his investment in Kansas
as well as see it become a free state.

Meanwhile Missourians were organizing the Platte
County Rifles, the Blue Lodges, and the Self-Defen-
sives, and sending armed bands of Border Ruffians
into the territory. One pro-slavery town was named
Atchison, after Senator David Atchison, who wrote,
"We are organizing to meet their organization. We
will be compelled to shoot, burn and hang, but the
thing will soon be over."

The conflict in Kansas lasted a long time. A pro-
slavery legislature backed by President Pierce passed

laws forbidding anti-slavery men to hold office, banning anti-slavery publications, and providing the death penalty for a man who helped a slave to escape. When Free State men replied by choosing their own legislature and passing their own laws, their governor was arrested for treason. In 1856 a posse marched on Lawrence with banners reading:

> Let Yankees tremble, abolitionists fall,
> Our Motto is, Give Southern rights to all.

Senator Atchison gleefully fired the first cannon shot at the Free State Hotel while his followers tossed newspaper presses into the river and burned down a large part of the town.

Most of the Free State men were not abolitionists, but here and there across the prairie a familiar face could be seen. Four nights after the burning of Lawrence, old John Brown, who had sworn an oath to end slavery, knocked on the doors of five pro-slavery men living along Pottawatamie Creek, hauled them outside, and killed them.

His violent deed became a turning point in the Kansas struggle. Free-Soilers who had begun to compromise in the hope that they would be left to live in peace stiffened their resistance and fought back. "I have no meat, no meal, no potatoes, no money to buy them, but I'll live or die in Kansas," one settler swore.

Two hundred men, women, and children were killed in skirmishes in Kansas in 1856, and crops, cattle, and horses valued at two million dollars were destroyed. The South won all the first battles. Bands of men crossed the border from as far away as Georgia and South Carolina. For a time they even had the U. S. Army on their side. But in the long pull the Free-Soilers not only had a better cause but better guns.

The guns were a brand-new product of Yankee industry—the Sharps breech-loading rifle which fired ten shots a minute. Far superior to any weapon the Missourians owned, they were the gifts of committees of respectable gentlemen in every Eastern state. Two hundred arrived in one week from Massachusetts, sixty-three from Connecticut, another hundred from New York. At first the rifles were nicknamed "Sharps' Rights of the People." Then the Reverend Henry Ward Beecher and his Brooklyn congregation presented each member of an emigrant party with a Bible and a Sharps. After that everyone called them "Beecher's Bibles."

Beecher's Bibles were shipped in crates labeled BOOKS or REVISED STATUTES so that they wouldn't be confiscated by the enemy on the way. After these camouflages failed, the Reverend Thomas Wentworth Higginson, who had "preached himself out of his pulpit" because of his anti-slavery views, led a group of armed settlers to Kansas Territory. Because the Missouri River towns and even the steamboats were controlled by Border Ruffians, Higginson was forced to go the long way around through Iowa, traveling the last hundred miles on foot.

So there was the Emigrant Aid Society and John Brown and Beecher's Bibles. But another part of the Kansas struggle took place in Washington. The ruins of the Free State Hotel in Lawrence were still smoking when Senator Charles Sumner rose on the Senate floor to talk about "The Crime against Kansas." Crowded galleries hung on his words as he denounced Southern leaders, slavery, and that "swindle," the Kansas-Nebraska Act. Two days later he was sitting at his desk in the Senate when Preston Brooks, a South Carolina congressman, struck him over the head with a cane. Unable to rise and defend himself because his long legs were pinned under the desk, Sumner was beaten into unconsciousness. Brooks's cane splintered into bits, but he kept right on striking the defenseless man.

As Sumner lay close to death, his brutal beating in the chamber of the United States Senate united the North as no other incident had done. Conservative men who disagreed with his anti-slavery views organized protest meetings not only in Boston and New York but in New Jersey, Michigan, New Hampshire, Iowa, Ohio. Letters poured in from ordinary people. "We are in great indignation here," a girl in Connecticut wrote. "I don't think it is of very much use to stay any longer in the High School, as the boys would better be learning to hold muskets, and the girls to make bullets."

In the South, Brooks became a hero. "Every Southern man sustains me," he wrote to his brother. "The fragments of the stick are begged for as sacred relicts." A GOOD DEED, the Richmond *Whig* headlined its story. "These vulgar abolitionists must be lashed into submission," the Richmond *Enquirer* thought. At the University of Virginia students collected money for a new cane for Brooks with "a heavy gold head, which will be suitably inscribed and also bear upon it a device of the human head, badly cracked and broken."

Sumner was unable to resume his Senate seat for three years, but his beating was another costly victory for the South. Public indignation linked "Bleeding Sumner" and "Bleeding Kansas" until the Ruffian army was forced to disband. Wagon trains of emigrants slowly settled the Great Plains. They learned how to chip holes in the frozen soil with axes, to plant their first corn. They milked cows they had brought with them and used their Sharps rifles to hunt rabbits and deer.

In 1858 they went to the polls and voted down slavery.

The Sword of Gideon

In firing his gun, he has merely told us what time of day it is. It is high noon, thank God!
—William Lloyd Garrison

Once upon a time every boy born in the United States was either a little Whig or a little Democrat. The two parties differed when they talked about tariffs or national banks, but they saw eye to eye on slavery. Neither was interested in bringing it to an end.

In the turbulent years before the Civil War both parties began to splinter into as many pieces as Congressman Brooks's cane. There were Cotton Whigs, Webster Whigs, Conscience Whigs. And Hunker Democrats, Barnburners, Anti-Nebraska Democrats, and just plain Southern Democrats. And a Liberty party, a Free-Soil party, and a Know-Nothing party which attacked immigrants, Catholics, and, sometimes, slavery.

With each new crisis, more and more men left their old parties. When the Fugitive Slave Law passed, a Brooklyn newspaper editor named Walt Whitman resigned from the Democrats and wrote a poem titled "Blood Money." "The scales fell from my eyes and I gave up the Whig party," Boston's wealthy banker, John Murray Forbes, said at almost the same moment.

The resentment against the Kansas-Nebraska Act brought fragments of the old parties together into a new one. Conscience Whigs, Barnburners, Anti-Nebraska Democrats, Free-Soilers met to form the Republican party. The name they chose was one that Thomas Jefferson had used many years earlier.

When Lawrence was burned and Sumner beaten, a lanky Illinois lawyer who had served a term in Congress as a Whig attended his state's first Republican convention. Thinking out loud, he gave his reasons for joining the new group:

"I read once in a law book, 'A slave is a human being who is legally not a *person* but a *thing*.' And if the safeguards to liberty are broken down, as is now attempted, when they have made *things* of all the free Negroes, how long, think you, before they will begin to make *things* of poor white men?

"Suppose Kansas comes in a slave state, and all the Border Ruffians have barbecues about it, and Free-State men come trailing back to the dishonored North, like whipped dogs with their tails between their legs, is it not evident that this is no more the 'land of the free'?"

Abraham Lincoln wasn't talking about emancipation for the slave. He wasn't asking for repeal of the Fugitive Slave Law or for support for the Underground Railroad. He was summing up his new party's program of "Free Soil, Free Labor, Free Men."

The program wasn't strong enough for abolitionists like William Lloyd Garrison and Wendell Phillips. They wanted slavery to end in South Carolina as well as in Kansas and Nebraska. Frederick Douglass was more optimistic, however. "We have turned Whigs and Democrats into Republicans and we can turn Republicans into abolitionists," he pointed out.

It took time, and many brave men's lives, before his prophecy came true.

The white South shrugged off the Republican party by becoming bolder than ever. Cotton was king. Seven eighths of the world's cotton was grown in the Southern states. Without it, factories would close down and workmen would starve all over the world. "We have only to shut off your supply of cotton for a few weeks," a planter told the London *Times* correspondent, "and we can create a revolution in Great Britain. Four million of your people are dependent on us for their bread."

King Cotton demanded the reopening of the African slave trade. "If it is right to buy slaves in Virginia and carry them to New Orleans why is it not right to buy them in Cuba, Brazil, or Africa, and carry them there?" an Alabamian asked. Slave ships fitted out in New York City were landing cargoes of salt-water Africans on the coast of Florida, Georgia, Texas. In 1859 Senator Stephen Douglas reported that "there had been more Slaves imported in the Southern States, during the last year, than had ever been imported before in any one year, even when the Slave trade was legal." The traders were sometimes caught by federal officers, but they were always allowed to go free while their victims were sold to the planters.

King Cotton demanded new land in Central America and the annexation of Cuba. If Spain should refuse to sell the island at "a fair price," spokesmen for the South declared, "we shall be justified in wresting it from Spain if we possess the power."

King Cotton clamped down tighter than ever on the liberties of its citizens. "We have got to hate everything with the prefix free," a Southern newspaperman wrote. "From free Negro to free will, free thinking, free children, and free schools—all belonging to the same brood of damnable isms." In the election of 1856 not one man in the cotton states dared to vote for the Republican party.

Only the black South voted that year—with their arms and their feet. Revolts were put down in North Carolina, Maryland, Alabama, Florida, Mississippi. Slaves working in the iron mills of Kentucky rebelled. In Texas they "killed off all the dogs in the neighborhood and were preparing for a general attack" when they were betrayed. A Georgia paper "refrained from giving our readers any of the accounts of contemplated insurrections" while the *Daily Picayune* in New Orleans hinted mysteriously at "a spirit of turbulence abroad in various quarters."

Business boomed on the Underground Railroad. Runaways were arriving in Philadelphia every day of the week. The Ohio branch was so busy that Kentucky slaveowners began to move their property away from the river towns. In Texas, rangers patrolled the Rio Grande to prevent fugitives from crossing over into Mexico.

New conductors joined the ranks. Alexander Ross, a distinguished Canadian scientist, made a trip through Georgia, South Carolina, and Mississippi. With field glasses slung over his shoulder and a notebook in his hand, he wandered across the fields studying rare birds and collecting interesting flowers. Impressed with the scholarly bird watcher, planters never discovered that his specimen bag contained pocket compasses and knives and his notebook, a coded list of Underground Railroad stations.

An entirely different kind of Underground Railroad operation took place when a Missouri slave slipped across the Kansas border to ask for help. His wife and children were about to be sold to Texas owners. On a frosty December night John Brown led an armed band into Missouri. With a revolver in his hand, he freed the man's family and seven other slaves. The raiders also took horses, wagons, and food "to the amount due to the Negroes" for their past services.

As the report of the raid traveled to Washington, President Buchanan added $250 to the $3000 reward Missouri's governor offered for the arrest of John Brown. Dodging posses, fighting off pursuers, Brown led his eleven fugitives across the frozen prairie from Kansas to Iowa and from Illinois to Michigan. It was spring when he arrived in Detroit to see his party safely aboard a ferry bound for Canada. There were twelve in the group by then, one of them a baby who had been named John Brown.

But freeing a score of slaves in Georgia or Missouri was "like an attempt to bail out the ocean with a teaspoon," Frederick Douglass said. There were still almost four million in the South and the long, long road to emancipation was leading in a new direction.

The Republicans had scarcely recovered from their defeat in the 1856 election when the Supreme Court handed down the Dred Scott decision. Dred Scott was a slave who sued for his freedom after his master took him to live in a free state for a time. The Court had a simple question to decide. Did his stay in a free state make Scott a free man? After denying liberty to Scott the judges went far beyond the answer to this question. Not only did Chief Justice Taney declare that the "rights of the Declaration of Independence do not relate to the Negro for whom citizenship is impossible" but he also found that "Congress has no power to abolish or prevent slavery in any of the territories."

Writing today, Supreme Court Justice William O.

Douglas has called the Dred Scott decision "probably the most unworthy, ill-advised opinion" in the Court's history. It meant that even if settlers in a territory voted against slavery Congress could not enforce their decision. It meant slavery not only in Kansas and Nebraska, but in all of the Western lands. If the decision stood unchallenged, it meant the loss of the whole struggle for free soil.

While the South called on citizens to respect the highest court in the land, Northerners attacked the Court and proposed its reorganization. A Chicago newspaper had "visions of coffle gangs on their way through Illinois. Chicago might become a slave market and men, women and children may be sold off the block in our streets."

Fighting for a seat in the Senate in the campaign of 1858, Abraham Lincoln warned that the Dred Scott decision could lead to slavery in every state "unless the power of the present political dynasty shall be met and overthrown." "A house divided against itself cannot stand. I believe this government cannot endure permanently half slave and half free," he said. ". . . I do not expect the house to fall—but I do expect it will cease to be divided."

The Republicans were gaining ground in every Northern state. At political meetings and in Congress there was less and less talk about compromise and more and more talk about disunion—and even war. But "These men are all talk," John Brown stormed. "What is needed is action!"

He was fifty-nine years old, shoulders stooped, sick with ague, his flowing beard turned white. He was a man who held morning and evening prayers with his family, who read from the Bible the stories of Gideon and his sword and of Samson, who brought down the temple of the Philistines even though it meant his own death. Often he said, "One man and God can overturn the universe."

He was such a man.

On the seventeenth of October 1859 telegraph wires vibrated with the news. "Fearful and Exciting Intelligence! Negro Insurrection at Harpers Ferry! Seizure of the United States Arsenal by the Insurrectionists! Troops despatched against the Insurgents!"

John Brown and twenty-one of his followers, five of whom were Negroes, had captured the government arsenal at Harpers Ferry, Virginia. Brown's plan was to start a slave rebellion, to lead an army of black men to the Alleghenies. With the mountains as their fortress, they would wage war on the South until all the slaves were free.

Soldiers marched on the little Virginia town from Washington, Baltimore, Fredericksburg. Battering down the arsenal door, they killed most of John Brown's band, including two of his sons. A young soldier beat Brown to his knees with his sword while another ran a bayonet through the body of the old man.

But John Brown lived for another six weeks. Too weak to sit up, he lay on a cot in a courtroom, listening to his trial for treason. When his wounds were healed he climbed the steps to the gallows and stood erect while a hangman fastened a rope around his neck.

In those last weeks of living and dying he came close to overturning the universe. Every word that he spoke, every letter he wrote was reported to an anxious country.

"I pity the poor in bondage that have none to help them. . . . I think I did right and that others will do right to interfere at any time. . . . Had I interfered in behalf of the rich, the powerful, the intelligent, or the so-called great, every man in this court would have deemed it an act worthy of reward rather than punishment. . . . You may dispose of me easily, but this question is still to be settled—this Negro question —the end of that is not yet."

Were these the words of a madman, as most people first assumed him to be? If so, "I thank God that one man is found who can go crazy for an idea," a Cincinnati minister said.

In those last weeks the simplicity and courage of the old man transformed him into a martyr who was giving his life for a cause in which others also believed. "An apostle and a hero," Victor Hugo wrote from France. "That new saint," Ralph Waldo Emerson called him, "who will make the gallows glorious like the cross."

There were rumors of rescue attempts. Plans were laid in Kansas, in Boston, New York, Ohio. But John Brown only shook his head. "I am worth now infi-

nitely more to die than to live. In no other possible way could I be used to so much advantage to the cause of God and humanity." Hundreds of soldiers

were posted around his jail, but only a cow approaching the guards one evening failed to give the countersign and was shot.

Arising at dawn on the day of his execution, he wrote a final message for his countrymen. "I, John Brown, am now quite certain that the crimes of this guilty land will never be purged away but with blood."

When they cut his body down from the gallows and brought him home to bury him, thousands wept. "He has abolished slavery," Wendell Phillips said at his grave. "True, the slave is still there. So, when the tempest uproots a pine it looks green for months—a year or two. Still, it is timber, not a tree. John Brown has loosened the roots of the slave system."

In the winter of his death the divided house swayed with each passing breeze. The jittery South now feared invasion as well as slave rebellion. Patrols halted New York businessmen and held them for questioning. In Georgia, Northerners traveling by boat were not allowed to land. Any one of them might be another John Brown who would succeed where he had failed.

There were violent scenes in Congress. Pro- and anti-slavery men advanced toward each other with clenched fists. Pistols were drawn, bowie knives brandished, and only the intervention of the sergeant-at-arms prevented pitched battles in the aisles.

In the Senate, Robert Toombs of Georgia blamed John Brown's raid on "the black Republican party." "It has already declared war against you and your institutions. It has already compelled you to arm for your defense. Defend yourselves!" he thundered.

The Republicans denounced Brown and denied

that they had any intention of interfering with slavery in the South. But the planters were raising two billion pounds of cotton that year. They would settle for nothing less than slavery in *all* the territories, guaranteed by the Constitution, for *all* time.

That summer, while supporters of Abraham Lincoln, Republican candidate for President, paraded down Fifth Avenue in New York singing, "Ain't You Glad You Joined the Republicans?" his opponents were buying guns. They paraded in Southern cities with rifles on their shoulders and banners proclaiming, "Resistance to Lincoln Is Obedience to God."

Lincoln won, and on Election Day the divided house began to fall. As soon as he had cast his vote for the Democratic candidate, Edmund Ruffin, Virginia planter and ardent disunionist, took a train for South Carolina. He carried with him one of the pikes John Brown had brought to Harpers Ferry. The pike was labeled "Sample of the Favors Designed for Us by Our Northern Brethren." Pike in hand, Ruffin sat on the platform when South Carolinians met to secede from the Union. "The time since I have been here has been the happiest of my life," he wrote to his son.

Mississippi, Florida, Alabama, Georgia followed South Carolina's example until there was a Confederate States of America, founded "upon the great truth that the Negro is not equal to the white man, that slavery is his natural and normal condition." Laying aside his pike, Edmund Ruffin joined the Palmetto Guard. Before dawn on April 12, 1861, he pulled the lanyard of a cannon in Charleston Harbor. A shell arched across the water to crash against the walls of Fort Sumter.

A year and a half after John Brown was hanged, a regiment of blue-coated Union soldiers marched to war singing:

"John Brown's body lies a-moulderin' in the grave,
But his soul goes marching on.
He captured Harpers Ferry with his nineteen men so
   true,
And he frightened old Virginia till she trembled through
   and through;
They hung him for a traitor, themselves the traitor crew,
But his soul goes marching on."

Ring, O Bells!

Without slavery the rebellion could never have existed; without slavery it could not continue.
—ABRAHAM LINCOLN

WHEN Frederick Douglass heard that Confederate troops had captured Fort Sumter he shouted, "God be praised!" To him, the rebellion of the slave states against the government of the United States could have only one end—the abolition of slavery. "The slaveholders themselves have saved our cause," he said. "They have exposed the throat of slavery to the keen knife of liberty."

Perhaps Abraham Lincoln thought so too. He had always hated slavery. Traveling on the Western rivers as a young man, the sight of "slaves shackled together with irons was a continued torment" to him, he said. At the height of Northern opposition to the Fugitive Slave Law he had written to a friend, "I confess I hate to see the poor creatures hunted down and caught and carried back to their stripes and unrequited toil; but I bite my lips and keep quiet."

But now Abraham Lincoln was President of the United States and Commander-in-Chief of its Army and Navy. His job was to preserve the Union. The day after Sumter fell he called for seventy-five thousand troops to put down the rebellion. As for slavery, he explained in his Inaugural Address that he did not propose "to interfere with the institution in the States where it exists."

In the first months of the Civil War, President Lincoln continued to bite his lips and keep quiet. He listened to men from Kentucky, Maryland, Missouri, Delaware, who had remained loyal to the Union and loyal to slavery. To New York merchants and bankers whose pro-slavery mayor, refusing to raise the Stars and Stripes over City Hall, proposed that New York secede to become a free city, so that it could continue to trade with the South. He heard soldiers marching across the Potomac bridge into Virginia singing:

"To the flag we are pledged, all its foes we abhor,
And we ain't for the Negro, but we are for the war."

Lincoln listened to anti-slavery congressmen—Radical Republicans they were called—who had an increasingly loud voice in the Senate and House now that Southern representatives had resigned. On one of Charles Sumner's first visits to the White House he urged the President to use his war powers to free the Rebels' slaves.

Lincoln listened patiently to everyone. "My policy is to have no policy," he told his secretary. "What I want is to get done what the people desire to have done, and the question for me is how to find that out exactly."

Oddly enough, it was the slaves themselves who began to shape a policy for the President. There were five million whites and four million slaves in the Confederate States. As long as the Negroes stayed on the plantations tending the crops, or worked on fortifications and harbor defenses, every able-bodied white man could join the Rebel Army. If the slaves stopped working, the Confederacy would be crippled.

The war was only two weeks old when the first slaves stopped working. Instead of riding the Underground Railroad to Canada they presented themselves at the nearest Union camp. To their dismay, they were promptly sent back to their owners. General George McClellan issued an order to his officers to crush any attempt at slave rebellion "with an iron hand."

The commander of the Union's Department of Virginia, Benjamin Butler, disagreed with McClellan's stand. A pro-slavery New Englander who had backed Jefferson Davis for the United States presidency, he could hardly be accused of being an abolitionist. He was, however, a practical man. When three husky slaves paddled across Chesapeake Bay to his camp he gladly put them to work building a bakehouse for his soldiers.

The next day the war in Virginia stood still for an

hour while a Confederate major with a flag of truce in his hand paid Butler a visit. Reminding him of his obligations under the Fugitive Slave Law, the major demanded the return of the runaways. Butler refused. Since the South had left the Union, slaveowners could hardly claim the protection of federal law, he pointed out. With a sly smile, he declared that the fugitives were "contraband of war."

The word "contraband" caught on immediately. Law-abiding citizens saw that it destroyed the last reason for obeying the Fugitive Slave Law. Politicians and army officers who were uncomfortable about calling runaway slaves free men spoke of them as "contrabands" in all official documents. Throughout the war newspapermen covering the battlefront consulted "the intelligent contraband" for information.

Most important of all, "contraband" was whispered, sung, tapped out on the grapevine telegraph. Two days after Butler's interview with the Confederate major, eight Negroes entered his lines. A day later, fifty-nine appeared. In two months, when his camp sheltered nine hundred contrabands, Congress drew up a law authorizing the confiscation of slaves whose owners permitted them to work on military installations. Confiscation didn't mean emancipation. The status of the runaways, particularly the women and children, was left undecided. But the shadowy outline of a policy toward slavery was beginning to appear.

Whenever Union soldiers marched into the South

—in tidewater Virginia, on the coast of South Carolina and the banks of the Mississippi—slaves stampeded to meet them. Along the Tennessee River
contrabands were "coming in by wagon loads." In
Alabama federal troops "were almost smothered by
welcoming blacks." After the capture of New Orleans
"the marching of a Union column into one of the sugar
parishes was like thrusting a walking stick into an
ant-hill." Hungry, ragged, carrying babies on their
backs, frying pans and quilts in their hands, they came
to join the Yankee soldiers.

By land and sea they came. When a Northern merchant vessel was captured by a Confederate privateer,
William Tillman, a Negro steward, killed the Rebel
officers who had been put aboard and sailed the merchantman to New York. Robert Smalls, a slave pilot,
stole a Confederate gunboat from Charleston Harbor. With a slave crew and their wives and children,
he set out before dawn one May morning. Giving the
proper signals as he passed the guns of Fort Sumter, he delivered the boat to the Union fleet. "I
thought it might be of some service to Uncle Abe,"
this "daring and intelligent contraband" said.

In the army camps the contrabands made themselves useful. Living in rude barracks with their families, they drew army rations of hardtack and salt beef,
and army laborers' pay. They built forts and dug
trenches, unloaded ships and railway cars. Many
served as wagon masters, teamsters, blacksmiths,
cooks while their wives washed uniforms and their

children crowded around the soldiers' campfires at
night, begging to be taught their ABCs.

The contrabands weren't welcomed everywhere by
Lincoln's generals. In the Department of the West,
Halleck refused to allow them to enter his lines. In
Tennessee, Sherman permitted runaways in camp,
but he also permitted their masters to look for them,
if the slaveowners swore loyalty to the Union. One
Massachusetts colonel attempted to please everyone
by putting runaway and owner outside his camp at
the same time. If the slave could outrun his master
he was free.

As he tried to steer a middle course, Abraham Lincoln sometimes found his anti-slavery generals more
troublesome than his pro-slavery ones. Fighting
against guerrilla raiders in Missouri, John C. Fré-
mont confiscated all Rebel property and gave Rebel-
owned slaves their liberty. David Hunter did the
same thing on the Sea Islands in South Carolina, but
Lincoln canceled the orders of both men, calling them
"a little too previous."

The President was listening more intently than ever
to learn what the people wanted him to do. The war
was going badly. His first call for troops had brought
a flood of men to recruiting offices. But fifteen months
later when he asked for 300,000 volunteers he heard
grumbles instead of cheers. Business was good. Wages
were rising. Besides, what was the war being fought
for, anyway?

Americans weren't the only ones to ask this question. Deprived of cotton by the Union blockade of Southern ports, mills had shut down in the textile districts of England and France. A million European workers were out of jobs. Employers talked of recognizing the South as a sovereign nation, even of entering the war on the side of the Confederacy. But the workingmen, including the unemployed mill hands, supported the Union, if—it was a big if—the Civil War would end slavery.

Lincoln was pulled first one way and then the other. The North needed soldiers, yet free Negroes whose ancestors had fought in the Revolution and War of 1812 were rejected by the War Department. "I have put thousands of muskets into the hands of Tennessee, Kentucky, and western North Carolina," the President said. "These men do not believe in mustering in the Negro. If I do it these thousands of muskets will be turned against us."

The North needed soldiers but feared to arm the slaves. "We are striking with our soft white hand, when we should be striking with the iron hand of the black man, which we keep chained behind us," Frederick Douglass wrote. Giving guns to slaves would be "the most terrible weapon in our armor. Is that an argument against its use?" Thaddeus Stevens, a Radical Republican congressman, asked.

"It would do no good to go ahead any faster than the country would follow," Lincoln wearily answered. "Sumner and the rest of you would upset our applecart altogether, if you had your way. We'll fetch 'em, just give us a little time."

Time passed. At Shiloh the Union suffered ten thousand casualties. In the Seven Days' Battles around Mechanicsville, fifteen thousand Yankee soldiers were wounded or killed. There was no doubt that a long, tough war lay ahead. "Let the Administration honestly seek to destroy slavery, Mr. President, and you will have no enemies left and no rebellion," Wendell Phillips said.

Once again the President shook his head. "We didn't go into the war to put down slavery, but to put the flag back. To act differently at this moment would not only weaken our cause but smack of bad faith. No! We must wait until every other means has been exhausted. This thunderbolt will keep."

Lincoln carefully explored "other means." He ordered strict enforcement of the law against the African slave trade, the statute that had been openly violated for fifty-five years. Five slave ships were captured and a sea captain from Maine, caught at the mouth of the Congo River with nine hundred Negroes on board, was condemned to death.

Prominent Northerners begged Lincoln to pardon the slave trader. Pen in hand, he read through the reprieve that had been drawn up for his signature. With almost a wail of despair he told a visitor, "You don't know how hard it is to have a human being die when you know that a stroke of your pen may save him." But he let the pen fall from his fingers, and for the first time in American history a kidnaper of Africans was hanged.

Lincoln proposed that the United States recognize the black republics of Haiti and Liberia, as England and France had done almost half a century earlier. Congress agreed, but the State Department warned that a Negro ambassador would hardly be acceptable in Washington society. Ignoring diplomatic channels, Lincoln sent a private message to the Haitian President couched in his own undiplomatic language—"I shan't tear my shirt if he sends a Negro here!" When a "rather dark" Haitian minister arrived, he was warmly received at the White House.

Lincoln went further. He called Border State leaders to a meeting and begged them to emancipate their slaves, with Congress footing the bill. He wrote to Central and South America, trying to find a country where the freed Negroes could emigrate. By birth and marriage, Lincoln was a Border State man. In 1862 he could not imagine black and white men living as equals in the United States.

His halfway measures failed. Border State legislatures refused to consider emancipation, and spokesmen for free Negroes and contrabands wouldn't hear of moving to a strange land. "The children of the black man have enriched the soil by their tears, and sweat, and blood," Robert Purvis wrote from Philadelphia. "Sir, we were born here and here we choose to remain."

Then Lincoln took a momentous step. He signed a

bill giving freedom to the three thousand slaves in the District of Columbia. Ever since 1800 when the federal government moved to Washington, men had petitioned Congress to end slavery in the District. Now the long petition fight was over. "It is the first installment of the great debt which we all owe to an enslaved race," Senator Sumner said.

There was still more to come. Congress appropriated money for schools for Negro children in Washington and allowed black men to be employed as mail carriers. A law freed slaves in all the territories and a new Confiscation Act gave liberty to Rebel-owned slaves who escaped to the Union Army. In the language of the day, the runaways were no longer "contrabands." They had been transformed into "freedmen."

As the news traveled southward a million dollars' worth of slave property disappeared in a single week in North Carolina. South Carolinians began to move their slaves to Texas, and Georgians complained that their losses from runaways would soon amount to fifteen million dollars.

One by one the props holding up slavery were being knocked down. "The events taking place seem like a dream," Frederick Douglass wrote. Nevertheless, victory was still far away. Volunteers were trickling into recruiting offices. A draft was bitterly opposed. Lincoln's ambassadors overseas reported a growing sentiment for recognition of the Confederate States.

Lincoln was still listening. "A man watches his pear-tree day after day, impatient for the ripening of the fruit," he explained. "Let him attempt to *force* the process and he may spoil both fruit and tree. But let him patiently *wait,* and the ripe pear at length falls into his lap."

In the summer of 1862 the patient man came to a decision. Whenever he could escape from White House visitors he walked across the lawn to the military telegraph office. Borrowing sheets of foolscap from the operators, he began to write "something special." He listened to the dot-dash-dot of the clicking keys. He stared out of the window. He stopped to read dispatches from the battle fronts. He wrote, crossed out, wrote again.

With the first short days of fall, husbandman Lincoln concluded that his pears were ripe at last. On the twenty-second of September he issued the "special" message he had been working on. Newspapers around the world headlined it:

HIGHLY IMPORTANT. A PROCLAMATION BY THE PRESIDENT OF THE UNITED STATES. ALL SLAVES IN STATES IN REBELLION ON THE FIRST OF JANUARY NEXT TO BE FREE.

In England a monster mass meeting of workingmen celebrated the news. In Washington brass bands serenaded the White House and the Cabinet held a party at Secretary Chase's. "They all seemed to feel a sort of new and exhilarated life," Lincoln's secretary noted. "They breathed freer. The President's Proclamation had freed them as well as the slaves. They gleefully

and merrily called each other abolitionists and seemed
to enjoy the novel accusation of appropriating that
horrible name."

The abolitionists were more sparing with their
cheers. With one hundred days to wait, the "cautious,
forbearing, hesitating, slow" President—"the tortoise,"

Wendell Phillips called him—might change his mind.
"How slow this child of freedom is being born!"
Charles Sumner exclaimed.

Lincoln continued to listen. Border state men

begged him to withdraw the Proclamation. Confederate congressmen threatened to hang all Union prisoners after January 1. But the War Department quietly lifted its ban on Negro soldiers. Before the hundred days were over the Louisiana Native Guards and the 1st South Carolina Volunteers, a company of ex-slaves, went into action. The 1st Kansas Colored

Regiment was drilling and Massachusetts and Rhode
Island were calling for dark-skinned volunteers.
Northerners who were prejudiced against Negroes
smiled at a popular rhyme:

> Some say it is a burnin' shame
> To make the Negroes fight,
> An' that the trade o' being kilt
> Belongs but to the white;
>
> But as for me 'upon me soul'
> So liberal are we here,
> I'll let Sambo be murdered in place o' meself
> On every day in the year.

When Congress convened in December a sober
President delivered his annual message on Capitol
Hill. "Fellow citizens," he warned the lawmakers, "we
cannot escape history." Three weeks later he signed
the Emancipation Proclamation.

For almost two hundred and fifty years slaves on
the North American continent had struggled to break
their chains. At last the world's first democracy had
caught up with its promise of liberty and equality
for all.

In the winter of 1865, as the war drew painfully to
a close, Congress approved a 13th Amendment to the
Constitution:

"Neither slavery nor involuntary servitude . . .
shall exist within the United States, or any place subject to their jurisdiction."

For the first time the Constitution mentioned the word "slavery." "It winds the whole thing up," the President said.

Joyous crowds, lighting their way with torches, paraded to the White House that night. When they called for Lincoln he came to the window. "The great job is ended," he said. "The occasion is one of congratulation, and I cannot but congratulate all present, myself, the country, and the whole world upon this great moral victory!"

In Massachusetts, John Greenleaf Whittier penned his last anti-slavery poem:

> It is done!
> Clang of bell and roar of gun
> Send the tidings up and down.
> How the belfries rock and reel!
> How the great guns, peal on peal,
> Fling the joy from town to town!
>
> Ring, O bells!
> Every stroke exulting tells
> Of the burial hour of crime.
> Loud and long, that all may hear,
> Ring for every listening ear
> Of Eternity and Time!

Note to the Reader

Except for the story of Kamba, every incident in this book is true and every quotation accurate. Our forefathers were often long-winded, however. To make the story move faster, I have taken the liberty of shortening quotations without in any case changing their meaning. In several instances I have also translated heavy dialect into more readable English.

The information in FOREVER FREE has come from the following sources:

GENERAL HISTORIES

Beard, Charles and Mary. *Rise of American Civilization.* Macmillan, 1936.

Bontemps, Arna. *Story of the Negro.* Knopf, 1951.

Franklin, John Hope. *From Slavery to Freedom.* Knopf, 1956.

Hughes, Langston, and Meltzer, Milton. *A Pictorial History of the Negro in America*. Crown, 1956.

Redding, J. Saunders. *They Came in Chains*. Lippincott, 1950.

U. S. Department of Commerce. *Historical Statistics of the United States*. U. S. Government Printing Office, 1961.

Wilson, Henry. *Rise and Fall of Slave Power in America*. 3 vols. James R. Osgood and Co., 1872.

Writers Program of WPA. *The Negro in Virginia*. Hastings House, 1940.

AFRICA AND THE SLAVE TRADE

Brown, Ina C. *The Story of the American Negro*. Friendship Press, 1957.

Dow, George F. *Slave Ships and Slaving*. Marine Research Society, 1927.

Du Bois, W. E. B. *The Suppression of the African Slave-Trade*. Social Science Press, 1954.

——. *Black Folk Then and Now*. Henry Holt, 1939.

——. *The World and Africa*. Viking, 1947.

Herskovits, Melville. *The Myth of the Negro Past*. Beacon, 1958.

Williams, Eric. *Capitalism and Slavery*. University of North Carolina Press, 1944.

EIGHTEENTH-CENTURY AMERICA

Becker, Carl. *The Declaration of Independence*. Knopf, 1951.

Farrand, Max. *The Fathers of the Constitution*. Yale University Press, 1921.

——. *The Framing of the Constitution*. Yale University Press, 1913.

Lancaster, Bruce. *From Lexington to Liberty*. Doubleday, 1955.

Lengyel, Cornel. *Four Days in July*. Doubleday, 1958.

Livermore, George. *An Historical Research Respecting the Opinions of the Founders of the Republic on Negroes as Slaves, as Citizens and as Soldiers*. Boston, 1862.

Malone, Dumas. *Jefferson the Virginian*. Little, Brown, 1948.

Mazyck, Walter. *George Washington and the Negro*. Associated Publishers, 1932.

Van Doren, Carl. *Benjamin Franklin*. Viking, 1938.

Wilkes, Laura E. *Missing Pages in American History*. n.p. 1919.

RUNAWAYS AND REBELS

Aptheker, Herbert. *A Documentary History of the Negro People in the United States*. Citadel, 1951.

———. *Essays in the History of the American Negro*. International, 1945.

———. *American Negro Slave Revolts*. Columbia University Press, 1943.

———. *To Be Free*. International, 1948.

Ball, Charles. *Slavery in the United States*. n.p. 1836.

Breyfogle, William. *Make Free*. Lippincott, 1958.

Brown, William Wells. *Narrative of William Wells Brown*. n.p., 1849.

Child, L. Maria. *The Freedmen's Book*. Ticknor and Fields, 1865.

Douglas, Marjory Stoneman. *The Everglades*. Rinehart, 1947.

Douglass, Frederick. *The Heroic Slave*. n.p. 1853.

Giddings, Joshua R. *The Exiles of Florida*. Follett, Foster and Co., 1858.

Johnson, James Weldon. *Black Manhattan*. Knopf, 1930.

Korngold, Ralph. *Citizen Toussaint*. Little, Brown, 1945.

Porter, Kenneth. "Florida Slaves and Free Negroes in the

Seminole War," *Journal of Negro History,* October
1943.

——. "Three Fighters for Freedom," *Journal of Negro
History,* January 1943.

——. "Relations between Negroes and Indians within the
Present Limits of the United States, *Journal of Negro
History,* July 1932.

——. *Abraham, Phylon,* 2nd quarter, 1941.

Sterling, Dorothy. *Freedom Train.* Doubleday, 1954.

Still, William. *The Underground Railroad.* Porter &
Coates, 1872.

Stowe, Harriet Beecher. *Dred.* Houghton Mifflin, 1888.

NEGRO LEADERS

Brawley, Benjamin. *Negro Builders and Heroes.* University of North Carolina Press, 1937.

Douglass, Frederick. *Life and Times.* Park Publishing Co.,
1882.

——. *Life and Writings,* ed. Philip Foner. Vols. I–III. International, 1952.

Graham, Shirley. *Your Most Humble Servant.* Messner,
1949.

Ottley, Roi. *Black Odyssey.* Scribner's, 1949.

Quarles, Benjamin. *Frederick Douglass.* Associated Publishers, 1948.

AMERICAN SLAVERY

American Anti-Slavery Society. *American Slavery as It Is.*
New York, 1839.

Bancroft, Frederic. *Slave-Trading in the Old South.* Furst,
1931.

Bauer, Alice and Raymond. "Day to Day Resistance to
Slavery, *Journal of Negro History,* October 1942.

Botkin, Benjamin A. *Lay My Burden Down.* University
of Chicago Press, 1946.

Frazier, E. Franklin. *The Negro Family in the United States*. Citadel, 1948.

Olmsted, Frederick Law. *A Journey in the Seaboard Slave States*. 2 vols. Putnam's, 1904.

Phillips, Ulrich B. *American Negro Slavery*. Peter Smith, 1959.

Stampp, Kenneth M. *The Peculiar Institution*. Knopf, 1956.

ABOLITIONISM
Buckmaster, Henrietta. *Let My People Go*. Harper, 1941.

Chapman, John Jay. *William Lloyd Garrison*. Doubleday, 1959.

Emerson, Ralph Waldo. *Miscellanies*, Houghton Mifflin, 1871.

Garrison, W. P. and F. J. *William Lloyd Garrison*. 4 vols. Houghton Mifflin, 1894.

Lader, Lawrence. *The Bold Brahmins*. Dutton, 1961.

Sherwin, Oscar. *Prophet of Liberty: The Life and Times of Wendell Phillips*. Bookman Associates, 1958.

Redpath, James. *The Public Life of Capt. John Brown*. Thayer and Eldridge, 1860.

Villard, Oswald Garrison. *John Brown*. Knopf, 1943.

U. S. POLITICS, 1830–60
Filler, Louis. *The Crusade against Slavery*. Harper, 1960.

Dumond, Dwight L. *Antislavery Origins of the Civil War*. University of Michigan Press, 1959.

Donald, David. *Charles Sumner and the Coming of the Civil War*. Knopf, 1960.

Stampp, Kenneth M., ed. *The Causes of the Civil War*. Prentice-Hall, 1961.

Weld, Theodore. *Letters*, ed. Dwight L. Dumond and Gilbert H. Barnes. D. Appleton-Century, 1934.

LINCOLN AND THE CIVIL WAR

Higginson, Thomas Wentworth. *Army Life in a Black Regiment*. Fields, Osgood & Co., 1870.

Leech, Margaret. *Reveille in Washington, 1860–1865*. Harper, 1941.

Newspaper clippings from the *Liberator*, the New York *Times*, Norfolk *Journal and Guide*.

Quarles, Benjamin. *The Negro in the Civil War*. Little, Brown, 1953.

Sandburg, Carl. *Abraham Lincoln, The Prairie Years*. 2 vols. Harcourt, Brace, 1926.

————. *Abraham Lincoln, The War Years*. 4 vols. Harcourt, Brace, 1939.

Sterling, Dorothy. *Captain of the Planter*. Doubleday, 1958.

Swanberg, W. A. *First Blood*. Scribner's, 1958.

Turner, Bishop H. M. *The Negro in Slavery, War and Peace*. A.M.E. Book Concern, 1913.

Washington, John E. *They Knew Lincoln*. Dutton, 1942.

Wilbur, Henry W. *Lincoln's Attitude towards Slavery and Emancipation*. Walter H. Jenkins, 1914.

POEMS AND SONGS

Allen, William Francis, Ware, C. P., and Garrison, L. M. *Slave Songs of the United States*. Peter Smith, 1951.

Ames, Russell. *The Story of American Folk Song*. Grosset & Dunlap, 1955.

Lowell, James Russell. *Poetical Works*. Houghton Mifflin, 1890.

Whittier, John Greenleaf. *Poetical Works*, Vol. III. Houghton Mifflin, 1895.

Work, John W., ed. *American Negro Songs and Spirituals*. Bonanza Books, 1940.